From Beyond the Skies

ENDORSEMENTS

"This is a remarkable story about impossible things becoming possible through love, perseverance, and the strength of community."
-Eliud Kipchoge
Marathon World Record Holder and Olympic Gold Medalist

"Juli's story reminds me that God will and does choose the most unlikely people and places to show up through. It inspires me to see and remember the impact, power, and *necessity* of not doing life alone!

"*From Beyond the Skies* dives deep into the suffering and fear Juli and her family went through during one of the hardest, scariest seasons of their lives; it dives even deeper into the healing, transformative power of having a community knit together by love, intentionality, and openness around you.

"Reading Juli's book reminds me how different life can look when you're surrounded by people who care. I needed that reminder.

"If you're seeking community and need to believe in the goodness of your fellow man again because you can't quite see it lately, *grab this book*."
-Albert Tate
Co-Founder and Lead Pastor, Fellowship Church
Monrovia, California

"In *From Beyond the Skies*, Juli Boit describes far more than the harrowing struggles her family endured prior to triumphant bone marrow transplants for her two Kenyan sons facing pain and early death from sickle cell disease. Hers is the story of how a life grounded in love can dare to be vulnerable to the unexpected as an essential path toward wholeness for herself, her family, and the community of support that surrounds her. We all need to face the unknown empowered by her invitation to the wonder of love."

-Dr. Joe Mamlin and Sarah Ellen Mamlin
AMPATH Kenya

"For years, I've had the grand privilege to watch God call Juli Boit to just take the next step in Love. And I have seen her, as well as Titus, do just that. Jesus once said, 'In this world you will have trouble, but take heart for I have overcome the world.' This true story of faith, hope, and love is one that shows as real as our troubles may be, they are not the end of the story. Your challenges may not be the exact same as Juli's remarkable story, but I trust through this you will be strengthened to take God's next step for you in Love."

-Tom Hughes
Co-Lead Pastor, Christian Assembly Church
Los Angeles, California
Author: *Down to Earth: How Jesus' Stories
Can Change Your Everyday Life*

"Juli's story is a gift to all who read it. It's a story of the brutality of love; how it is a mess and a burden and a great invitation, all in one. Juli's story is a reminder that love looks like saying "yes" when it is scary, saying "yes" when it's shrouded with uncertainty. Love is being interruptible, as Juli and her husband demonstrate when they said yes to bringing a premature baby boy into the fold of their family. As Juli said, 'We had a choice, and it wasn't necessarily that there was a right or wrong way. But there was a yes and a no. There was a stopping to pay attention, interrupting our plans and the way we imagined our family would grow, as we chose to affirm Ryan's worth, to discern and discover—one day at a time—what it meant to love.' Love is a privilege that is both hard and holy. As you read her story, Juli's grief will become yours. You will find yourself in tears at times as she shares her pain and her questions in their rawest state. You will likewise share in her joy as you see God and others show up in her story to embrace her in the love and support her story is defined by."

–Blythe Hill
CEO/Founder, Dressember Foundation

FROM BEYOND THE SKIES

AN INVITATION INTO THE WONDER OF LOVE

JULI BOIT

NEW YORK

LONDON • NASHVILLE • MELBOURNE • VANCOUVER

FROM BEYOND THE SKIES

An Invitation into the Wonder of Love

Published in New York, New York, by Morgan James Publishing. Morgan James is a trademark of Morgan James, LLC. www.MorganJamesPublishing.com

This work depicts actual events in the life of the author as truthfully as recollection permits and/or can be verified by research. All persons within are actual individuals; there are no composite characters. The names of some individuals have been changed to respect their privacy.

All Scripture quotations, unless otherwise indicated, are taken from The Holy Bible, New International Version®, NIV®.

ISBN 9781631954276 paperback
ISBN 9781631954283 eBook
ISBN 9781631954290 audio
Library of Congress Control Number: 2020950540

Cover Design by:
Drew Shafer
www.drew-shafer.com

Interior Design by:
Chris Treccani
www.3dogcreative.net

Vector Children on cover by:
Estudio Maia
www.shutterstock.com

Morgan James is a proud partner of Habitat for Humanity Peninsula and Greater Williamsburg. Partners in building since 2006.

Get involved today! Visit
MorganJamesPublishing.com/giving-back

For our children
and all who walked beside us

TABLE OF CONTENTS

FOREWORD

When my Kenyan friends wanted to introduce me to Juli in March of 2007, I am embarrassed to say that I had low expectations for our relationship or for the work in which she was engaged. At that point, as a pediatrician and an HIV researcher, I was deeply immersed in the challenge of trying to scale-up an HIV care system across western Kenya with my colleagues at Moi University. My guiding question was how to provide long-term access to HIV treatment for the hundreds of thousands of families living with HIV in western Kenya and beyond.

I was doubtful that some Christian white woman living in a village in Kenya would have much to do with that big goal—even if I, too, was Christian and white and American and a woman.

Although I grew up in the Christian church, my encounters with American Christians in Kenya and the US very often left me wondering what it meant to be a follower of Jesus. I saw many groups of American Christians drop into Kenya for short periods of time on mission trips, and it was difficult to see the impact that they had on the HIV crisis gripping my heart. Almost every day, I was seeing desperate parents bring their dying children to our clinics. And even though there were medicines available to prevent or treat HIV and the other infections killing these children for only a few dollars, we were struggling mightily to make those accessible to families. Personally, I wrestled to keep my heart soft and open when it kept breaking over these children again and again.

I had a lot of questions for God. And I did not see the church doing much to even acknowledge the devastating deaths of one million more lives lost to HIV every year.

But, I have to tell you what it is like to meet Juli. When you first meet Juli, you are struck by a strong, deep beauty that radiates from her. This is not because she is physically beautiful, though she absolutely is, but the only words I have ever been able to use to describe Juli's beauty are that her love for God somehow radiates out of her and hits you as a deep beauty. I do not talk about God very often with people, but I have used those words to describe Juli at least a dozen times over the years that I have known her.

In her story here, Juli says that the question "What does it look like to love in this situation?" has become her guiding principle. Juli's life work to build a community that embodies that active love is the best antidote to my questions about the role of the church. And that love shimmers around her.

Of course, I was completely, deeply wrong about Juli's impact. Not only did she become integrated into the work of the AMPATH partnership in which I was working to provide a system for HIV care across Kenya, but her Kimbilio Hospice became a critical resource for many of the children in my care over the years. The Kimbilio Hospice and Care Center is not only a haven for dying patients but also the place where I can send my most broken or malnourished or neglected children. Most of the phone calls from me at the hospital to Juli in the village have started with, "I don't know what else we can do for this child. Do you think you could help?" Kimbilio is where we send those in need of the constant, slow, loving care that is often more than families or orphanages or even the hospital can provide. Kimbilio means "refuge" in Kiswahili. Juli and I have struggled and cried over deaths and losses together, but I have also seen this place of refuge bring many of our "hopeless" patients back to life.

Both Juli and Kimbilio have helped me through my own personal struggle with how to do this often heart-breaking work and keep my heart soft. In this story, Juli describes some of the healthcare workers at UCLA as "straddling the invisible line between getting a job done, which was essential, and loving their patients, which was kind and brave." Juli is brave like this as a nurse practitioner, and she has helped me learn how to straddle that line as an HIV physician as well.

When I tell the story of what our partnerships do in Kenya, I try to describe how we face broken systems and broken bodies and do what we can to enter in, to come alongside, to care, to help. Both Juli and Dr. Joe Mamlin have taught me that this is love, and I am thankful.

Now, Juli has written down the story of what it looked like for her and Titus to embody this same love and live it out in their family. Again, Juli is my teacher as I walked through each page considering what it looks like to live out this active, brave love as a mother. As a pediatrician, I was there with her in all the medical chaos. As a mother, I was there with her in the grief, the joy, and the devastation. Again, I am thankful.

No matter who you are as you come to this story, I think you will feel the radiant love beaming out on every page. *Karibu*—welcome in.

-Rachel Vreeman, MD, MS
Chair of the Department of Global Health
Professor of Pediatrics, Icahn School of Medicine at Mount Sinai
Director, Arnhold Institute for Global Health

Nothing could have prepared
Your heart to open like this.

From beyond the skies and the stars
This echo arrived inside you
And started to pulse with life,
Each beat a tiny act of growth,
Traversing all our ancient shapes
On its way home to itself.

Once it began, you were no longer your own.

~ John O'Donohue[1]

---

1   John O'Donohue, *To Bless the Space Between Us: A Book of Blessings* (New York: Doubleday, 2008), 56.

WHERE THIS STORY BEGAN

"If we ever write a book," Joe mentioned as he sipped from a bottle of room-temperature Coca-Cola, "we'd call it: *Only Love Matters.*"

We sat side by side at a rickety desk on a cool and wet Friday morning in a rural HIV clinic in Western Kenya. A line of men and women began to crowd the hallway, waiting for their turn to see the doctor.

The collective suffering that filled the space was immense. While the stories resembled one another, Dr. Joe paid careful attention to the details of each patient as if he or she were his brother or sister, his son or daughter before us. The reason was simple, and he said with perfect clarity, "She is my sister. He is my brother. As long as I remember that, everything else makes sense."

"The first chapter of the book would read: Only love matters," he continued. "All other chapters would repeat the same message. Only love matters. Only love matters. Only love matters."

He talked of this book outline often when we met and always finished by saying, "We'll never write the book, Juli. There are too many other important things to do. But we both know what it needs to say," and I joined in, "only love matters."

For more than ten years, I sat beside Joe most Friday mornings, listening to him tell the same stories each week, watching him thoughtfully envision and finally build an HIV program far reaching in its scope.

All the while, with great skill and intention, he cared for the person in front of him.

I met Dr. Joe Mamlin by chance—or more likely providence—months after moving to Kenya. I was a twenty-five-year-old nurse practitioner weary of watching people die alone from a treatable disease. In the rural village where I lived, we didn't have access to testing or treatment for HIV/AIDS. What we *did* have were wasting bodies, funerals, and orphans aplenty.

I showed up on a Friday morning in January 2005 to a one-room clinic about ten miles from where I was living. There, I found a seventy-year-old white man in the doorway who simply introduced himself to me as Joe. He held a green patient file in hand, ready to call the name printed on the front.

"What are *you* doing in the middle of nowhere?" he asked me in a thick North Carolina accent.

"I live close by," I explained. "My neighbor is terribly sick. I brought him to the clinic to see if there might be help available. Honestly, I'm tired of watching people die."

"I know exactly how you feel," he said. "Let me show you something." Joe ushered me into a room filled with HIV test kits, nutritional support, and antiretroviral drugs, but all I saw was hope.

That Friday, Joe—a humble professor of medicine from Indiana University whose idea of retirement involved building one of the largest and most successful HIV-treatment programs in the world—became my mentor and my friend.

Joe taught me how to dream impossible dreams but also how to love in tangible ways. I didn't know then how much that love would be tested and tried beyond what I thought I was capable of.

That it would take me across two continents and into the heart of my darkest fears and deepest longings.

This book is my attempt to put words to a far-fetched tale that, somehow, has become my real-life story. It is my account of a nearly three-year ordeal that spanned the space between my village in Kenya and Los Angeles; between the pediatric unit at UCLA and our home-away-from-home with dear friends who became family; between life and death with three children who would become more my own with each passing day. It was a journey that challenged my notions of love and invited me to experience its depths in ways I never thought possible.

Along the way, I took notes to remember and to process. In between our long stays in the hospital, especially, I'd wake up early in the morning, cup of hot tea in hand, to read and reread my notes, taking the time to ponder it all.

In those rare, quiet moments of many a morning, I wrote the words that have become this book. It was written with the hope to bear witness to the wonder and mystery of love. To tell my children a story they are likely to one day forget.

This is my account, though I recognize it's not solely my own to tell. It feels deeply important to me to honor the lives of the people who play a part in this story and the communities in both Kenya and Los Angeles who welcomed my family and me and allowed us to belong.

My hope is this book rightly reflects the beauty and complexity of the people I've come to love and the life I've been honored to live in Kenya.

Like Joe faithfully taught me, love is the only thing that really matters. While nothing could have prepared my heart to open like it has, an invitation from beyond the skies was extended my way.

In the words of Mary Oliver, "Instructions for living a life. Pay attention. Be astonished. Tell about it."[2]

---

2 Mary Oliver, *Red Bird* (Boston: Beacon Press, 2009).

1

When Stories Collide

t was a summery December afternoon when I first walked the dusty path leading to Kibet's home. No feelings of Christmastime filled the air. Varying hues of brown were replacing the brilliant shades of green that had covered the rolling hills only a few months prior when I first moved to the village of Kipkaren. And the vast fields that had been bursting with maize now lay bare and dormant, waiting for rain, waiting for the hope of a new season.

The rushing sound of the Kipkaren River grew louder as I entered Kibet's compound. A neighbor had requested I go and check on the man with *ugonjwa*, the sickness.

Everyone assumed it was AIDS, but no one uttered the word. There was still too much stigma and fear.

I had left my job as a nurse on an HIV unit in Los Angeles to come and work in Kenya. By now, HIV was mostly being treated as a chronic disease in the United States. In Kenya, we couldn't even say the word out loud, let alone have access to testing or treatment.

No one should die alone. This was one of the convictions that led me to leave my home and family to move to Kenya. Though still convinced it was true, I was also wrestling more and more with the day-to-day reality that no one should die of a preventable and treatable disease. Not because of poverty or geography, nor any other reason.

To reach Kibet's home, I followed a narrow path that led through a small grove of banana trees. In the shade of one of these trees, a hen rested from the hot sun while her chicks chirped rhythmically, hiding beneath her wings.

"*Hodi*," I said to announce my arrival.

A woman's voice gently replied, "*Karibu.*" Welcome. It was Kibet's wife, Karemi. As we greeted one another, I noticed a man sleeping quietly under the shade of a nearby tree.

Without introduction, I knew him to be Kibet.

Kibet was covered with a heavy, colorful woolen blanket. His feet extended well beyond the length of the foam mattress on which he was lying. His body was ravaged by untreated disease, and little more than a skeletal frame remained.

Surprised by my company, Kibet woke up and asked for a drink of water. I raised a metal cup to his lips as he gently sipped. In that moment, I knew how the story would go—or so I thought.

I would make routine home visits to care for Kibet and Karemi. Within weeks, Kibet would die. Without a proper diagnosis. Without an option of treatment.

The community would gather for Kibet's burial, and the problem of AIDS would go on in its destructive and unchallenged pattern.

* * *

My journey to Kenya began when I was a junior in nursing school, when a friend convinced me to accompany her to a meeting she didn't want to attend alone. The goal of the meeting was to share information about upcoming summer service opportunities. I had no intention of traveling, but I agreed to go to the meeting.

That summer, I found myself in villages in the west of Kenya without my friend. In those villages, I listened and learned each day from remarkable Kenyan leaders who cared about the suffering of their people. I saw the realities of AIDS within the context of a village setting.

There, troubling statistics took on a new meaning to me. Numbers became young people with names and stories. All of whose lives mattered.

Back in Los Angeles, after graduating, I began to work nights as a nurse on an HIV unit while studying in a nurse practitioner program. The AIDS crisis in Kenya still gripped me.

I didn't pretend to think I would be able to fix it, but I wondered if there were a space for me to help in some way or another.

And then a friend introduced me to a group of Kenyans living in Los Angeles. They were young adults from a middle-class, urban, educated background, just like me. They were trying to find their way in a new place and culture.

We talked about every topic under the sun, including many a conversation about the effects of colonialism and the damage done to their country and to their culture by "well-intentioned, white people."

My friends also called out the stereotypes and generalizations by which they were so often identified in America.

In those conversations I came to appreciate Kenya as much more than a faraway land where "poor-but-happy" people lived. It was neither a place to be pitied nor to be worshipped. Kenya rightfully grew to be more than my limited perception from experiences within a specific people, place, and time.

I listened and made room for complexity and for questions without simple answers.

And when in 2004 an opportunity came up for me to work with a nonprofit, community-based HIV program in the village of Kipkaren, I humbly said yes.

It didn't feel like a huge leap to go for a year or two; rather, it was just the next step.

* * *

The February 2001 edition of *Time* magazine featured a haunting photograph of an African child nestled against her grandmother. The child was wasted from disease. I remember that gut-wrenching cover and the impact it had on me like it was yesterday.

The words beside the image read: *Look at the pictures. Read the words. And then try not to care.*

The story stated: "Africa can provide no treatment for those with AIDS."[3]

Until the day I met Joe, I had wrongly believed those words.

On that Friday morning in 2005, I was sitting next to Kibet and Karemi when Joe told them they were HIV positive. "I've seen many people as sick as you return to life. If you'll take your medicine, you will be strong and fat again."

As we wrapped up our visit, Joe shared with me that while he knew how to build clinics and to treat patients, he was struggling to mobilize the sick from rural villages. Like Kibet and Karemi, patients from those villages didn't arrive at his clinics until it was almost too late.

Joe wrestled with questions of how to get testing and treatment to the people earlier. His concern was not for the few but the masses.

The events of the day were still reeling through my mind as I relayed them to David Tarus, a colleague, friend, and the leader of our village that evening. David lived by the Kalenjin parable, which says that a leader is not greater than his community.

I sat by the light of a kerosene lantern and shared a simple meal of vegetables and ugali—the staple cornmeal cake of Kenya—with David and his family. When it came to the HIV pandemic, David understood all too well the destructive effects of the virus on his people.

Discovering the existence of the HIV clinic presented an opportunity for David and our team to respond with urgency and full commitment as a powerful link with the rural communities Joe could not reach.

---

3   Johanna McGeary, "Death Stalks a Continent," *Time* magazine, February 12, 2001, http://content.time.com/time/world/article/0,8599,2056158,00.html.

That night, we started speaking of *ukimwi*, HIV/AIDS, calling out the disease for what it was. Open and honest discussion paved the way for HIV testing to enter the village. When it did, David Tarus was among the first in line to be tested. Hundreds followed his example.

For those who tested positive, treatment was available.

* * *

I moved to Kipkaren understanding, at least on the surface, what village life was like. There was no electricity or running water. Showers came in the form of buckets filled with river water, which changed in color depending on whether it was rainy season or not. Most toilets were a pit latrine. Drinking water came either from shallow wells in the community or the river—both needing to be carried in buckets and then boiled. To boil the water or to cook any food, firewood was collected. And clothes were washed in the river by hand.

Thankfully, there were women in the community who taught me the ropes and helped me in areas I was completely inept.

I lived in a small, round house with green iron sheeting as a roof. There was no internet access, and cell phones were just beginning to find their way into the village. I walked almost everywhere I needed to go—to the clinic or on home visits with our health team. To assist a mama to deliver her baby. To church, the market, or to visit a friend. To say *pole*, I'm sorry, when someone in the community lost a loved one to death.

All of this was doable for me.

While I am not overly adventuresome, I could survive—perhaps even thrive—in a place that at times felt a million miles away from home.

What was harder were the raw, unfiltered moments when one too many losses piled on top of one another. The nights I sat in a dark house by myself and wrestled with unanswerable questions from the day:

> *How do you tell an unsuspecting thirteen-year-old girl that she just tested positive for HIV?*
>
> *How do you respond to the cries of a mama who comes to your home early in the morning asking for assistance with school fees for her son?*
>
> *How do you encourage the dreams of an orphan who longs for an opportunity to go to college?*
>
> *What do you say to the barefooted street child who is eating a rotten tomato and asking you for bread?*
>
> *When a man with no hands and feet, sitting by the side of the road, says, "Nisaidie"—Help me—what do you do?*

* * *

On his first visit to the clinic, Kibet barely had enough strength to stand on a scale, let alone walk. His six-foot-three-inches frame weighed a meager ninety pounds.

After swallowing his daily cocktail of *dawa*—his anti-HIV medications—Kibet's appetite began to return. Eventually, his strength followed. His immune system slowly picked up, giving it a chance to fight again.

After a few months, Kibet and many others from our community were experiencing the Lazarus effect, just as Joe had hoped and predicted. People who had looked dead were coming back to life.

When I visited Kibet at his home, he told me about the first day we met. "When I woke up and saw you, I thought I was dying and you were an angel sent by God to take me to heaven," he said.

"There are not so many white people around here, you know, especially ones that would come to visit me in my home. You spoke words of hope, and when I finally realized I was not dead but still alive, I began to believe God loved me enough to send you to take care of me."

I sat quietly reflecting on Kibet's words, grateful that God loved us both enough to allow our stories to collide.

* * *

Five years later, I was still living in Kipkaren, working alongside a small but committed team of Kenyans who were passionate about the holistic care we provided to our patients and their families. In turn, I was offered rich hospitality by my Kenyan neighbors.

They taught me invaluable lessons about what it means to live in a community. Neighbors welcomed me into their homes of mud and thatch, always offering a cup of sweetened chai that smelled of smoke from the firewood over which it had been prepared. The fragrance had come to feel like home to me, like it held a collective memory of a thousand other cups shared before me.

All the while, a dream was rising within me to build a hospice to serve patients with advanced cancer and HIV/AIDS in Western Kenya.

In 2009, I founded Living Room International.[4] Soon after, we built a twenty-four-bed inpatient facility and called it Kimbilio, meaning *refuge* in Swahili. It would be located directly across the path from Kibet's home.

Kibet was a member of the construction team and pushed a wheelbarrow similar to what others had used to carry him around the village back when he was too weak to walk.

There have been plenty of days I looked toward Kibet's home and remembered: *There is more at work than I can see.*

In those moments filled with despair and grief, I recall all those years ago when I walked down a dusty path and could only perceive barren fields and a dying man. Buried in the dirt and pain, there was more at work. It's like God was hidden there.

I loved the life I was living in a village where my footprints blended daily with those of barefooted children on dirt paths, where a strange mixture of beauty and brokenness, joy and pain permeated the land.

But there was another dream rising within me, one I hadn't put words to yet and wouldn't for a while. While my role with HIV patients was exhausting, rewarding, and sometimes all-consuming, I wanted to experience what it was like to hold, nurture, and love a child of my own.

I wanted to be a mama.

---

4   In 2009, Living Room International was founded in an effort to meet the holistic needs of seriously ill adults and children and to provide life-giving and transformative refuge for thousands of people in Kenya. Today, Living Room has more than 100 skilled and loving Kenyan staff who care for the guests at our two hospices/hospitals in Western Kenya, manage our home-based care program, and run our funeral home.

2

Becoming a Mama

Los Angeles, California
September 2017

"How many children do you have?" a middle-aged nurse in navy-blue scrubs asked from the other side of his glass-paned window. I half-smiled knowing he was asking for a number, not an explanation. After all, the answer should be as easy to give as adding two and two.

"Uh, four?" I was not making it up but felt unsure of the right answer.

The nurse looked up from his form. "Have you traveled outside of the United States in the last thirty days?"

"Yes."

"In Africa?"

"Yes." I cringed at the red flags.

My baby was sick. Again. Ryan's fragile seventeen-month-old body was familiar with pain and suffering. This was the reason we traveled ten thousand miles, landing on US soil only thirty-six hours before. It was why we had left our home and work in Kenya. Ryan's high fever combined with his underlying sickle cell disease set off a domino effect of emergency services.

I joined Ryan on the narrow ER stretcher as antibiotics and IV fluids flowed into his veins. A second nurse resumed the list of questions on the intake form. "Does your house have a smoke detector?" she asked. This one caught me off guard, and I laughed nervously.

A series of plane rides landed us far away from our beloved Kenya. "Uh, no. We live in a village." A rule follower by nature, I once again felt the need to explain but paused instead. *Where would I even begin?*

Many of our neighbors didn't have electricity or running water in their homes. Fire departments with blaring sirens and red engines? Those were a few hours' drive from the village. And where most neighbors depended on the river for their supply of water, fire hydrants would be ludicrous. In fact, Ella, my then three-year-old, yelled, "Snowman!" every time she saw a fire hydrant during our last visit to the US. Maybe it had something to do with Olaf.

"No, we do not have a smoke alarm."

"How many children do you have?" The hard question resurfaced. While *many* wasn't an acceptable answer, it still seemed most appropriate.

My thoughts wandered to a women's health course I took in nursing school where we learned medical shorthand to narrate the number of pregnancies, births, and abortions. When charting on a patient, we'd write P3, G3, A0. (This meant 3 pregnancies, 3 live births, and 0 abortions—spontaneous from miscarriage, or otherwise.)

In my case, there was one pregnancy, one live birth. No miscarriages. One adoption. I was a legal guardian to two of the adopted baby's siblings and helped care for five more of their siblings, all still in Kenya.

Was there shorthand for that?

* * *

My practice at being a mama has been lifelong. Among my earliest memories was Christmas 1983. I was four years old, and like every other little girl in America, I wanted a Cabbage Patch Kid—you know, the dolls whose appeal reached far and wide and sold out in every department store across the country.

At the time, Amazon and eBay were still years from existing, and shopping frenzies entailed going to every Walmart and Toys "R" Us within driving distance.

Part of the draw of these dolls was their supposed uniqueness along with the story of how each needed a loving home into which they could be adopted. They came complete with a name—something like Edwin Nicholas or Cora Delilah—along with an adoption certificate for the new parent.

On Christmas morning, I was not at all disappointed when I opened a package to receive a homemade version of a Cabbage Patch Kid. My Granny Reba had fashioned mine with a plastic head, fabric body, and yarn hair—much like the real ones. Countless hours were spent practicing my mothering skills. Like my mom was to me, I was a good mama to that baby.

* * *

At Kimbilio, I cared for sick and dying men, women, and children. It was not unusual for mamas to ask our team to make sure their little ones would be alright after they were gone. Each request bearing the weight of a mother's love. We listened—our faces often stained with tears—and tried to assure them we would do whatever possible to help.

Parentless children were also brought to the hospice hungry, sick, and in great need of love. Our team picked these babies up and held them tight. Diapers were changed. Songs were sung in lovely garden spaces. We fed the little ones, spoon by spoon or drop by drop, until they were ready to do it for themselves. We celebrated victory. We celebrated life. And if our work was to care for them as they took their final breath, we grieved their death.

This had been my practice. My calling. My home for nearly a decade in Kenya. I loved my life, yet I ached for a family to call my own. My longing to be a wife and a mother was deep and wide.

At thirty-two, I was introduced through friends to a kind and gentle soul, a man named Titus, whose presence made me feel safe and alive. He grew up and lived only twelve miles away from Kipkaren. We fell in love over shared meals, visits to Titus' beautiful family farm, and on walks along the Kipkaren River.

Every time Titus showed up at my door, much patience, persistence, and maneuvering had been required, as the main highway leading to Kipkaren was under construction, and there was no easy way to get to me. He'd smile at me, flowers in hand, like the arduous journey was no big deal.

On my thirty-third birthday, we were on top of a mountain overlooking a magnificent rain forest. There, Titus asked me to marry him. It was an easy yes for me.

As Titus and I were preparing for our wedding, I mentioned to David Tarus that I didn't need a *koita,* a traditional engagement party. Anywhere from hundreds to even thousands of neighbors would attend such an event. I wanted something simple. I wanted to be selfless, I thought.

David looked at me and said firmly, "Well, Juli, it isn't about you. You belong to a community now, and they will want to come together to celebrate with you."

This was yet another major teaching moment for me—one of many over the years. Titus and I, along with our families, friends, colleagues, neighbors, friends of neighbors, and neighbors of friends celebrated our engagement on a rainy day in April. No invitation was required to attend. All were welcome. More than two thousand showed up.

Titus' family negotiated with David and the elders from our community over a dowry price, including cows and sheep. And then they anointed one another with oil as a symbol of our families becoming one.

This was about more than Titus and I being joined together. The *koita* symbolized our communities uniting, as well.

The celebrations continued with a small wedding ceremony with our family and friends in the US, followed by a Kenyan wedding with five thousand of our closest family and friends in attendance.

On our wedding day

Fourteen months later, Titus and I, along with our entire community, awaited the arrival of our baby girl.

* * *

There is a well-known African proverb that says, "It takes a village to raise a child." To our village, this is more than a proverb. It is a way of life. Children are seen to be the joy and responsibility of all.

Any elderly woman in society automatically becomes *koko*, or grandmother, to all children. The grandmother figure and the child both call each other *koko* as a term of endearment. The same is true for grandfather figures, using the word *agui*.

In another teaching moment, David Tarus told me I should know by name all my neighbors within a three-mile radius of where we live, along with the names of their children and their animals. He wasn't joking either.

There are flaws in our community, but there are also safety measures still in place, passed on from one generation to the next—nuanced traditions that promote belonging and safety for children.

* * *

During my pregnancy, I prepared for labor, believing a woman's body inherently knows what to do to deliver her baby. I've assisted in and witnessed many home and clinic births in the village. Many mamas struggle silently through the pain, far away from the safeguards of a hospital. Most of those births were without issues, the mamas surviving the epic task of birthing a tiny human.

For those who gave birth at the clinic, after a few hours they'd drink *uji*—a thick, corn-based porridge—wrap the baby in no fewer than six layers of clothes and blankets, and slowly make their way home on foot, baby in arms.

Giving birth is a process of breathing and writhing with moments of respite between the contractions. As the body opens—a process that feels mostly like death—it leads to new life. After much waiting and aching comes the releasing. An exhausted mama is rewarded with her baby nestled into her chest. Love in its purest form.

This was how it was supposed to go, at least according to the *Bradley Method* book Titus and I studied in the weeks leading up to my due date. Since no birthing classes were available to sign up for in Eldoret—the nearest town—this was our attempt at preparedness. Titus took it very seriously, poring over the book line by line in the same way he liked to read any and all instruction manuals.

I was ten days past my due date when my doctor phoned to tell me he wanted to induce me. I asked for one more day, hoping to let my body do its own laboring thing.

My younger brother Josh—whom we lovingly refer to as Uncle Mosh—was living with Titus and me at the time. He had needed a break and change of scenery, so a couple of months earlier, Josh quit his music editing job in Los Angeles and found his way to us.

On that overdue day, I forced him to walk what felt like a hundred miles along the dirt paths. I can only imagine what the neighbors thought as the *wazungu* duo, the white folks—especially the overly pregnant one—kept passing by, waving and greeting each time, as expected.

"*Ochamagei? Oyaenei?*" How are you? What are you doing? they'd ask over and again.

"*Chamagei. Kibendoti kityo.*" We are fine. Just walking. In other words, don't mind us.

I'm pretty sure we were the talk of the village that night, but it worked. Not that I can prove it was the walking that did the job, but the contractions began, strong and steady, at around ten that night while Titus, Josh, and I were crowded around a laptop watching a downloaded episode of *So You Think You Can Dance*.

By midnight, we were on our way to the hospital, over the hills and through the valleys. There are no streetlights in the village, and Titus was aware of each bump leading toward the main road.

Josh sat next to Titus as his wingman, and Allison—my dearest friend whom we picked up along the way—sat next to me as mine.

My head leaned forward. I took deep breaths as the contractions continued in the dark of night along the bumpy road. The thought consuming my mind was that the next time we'd be on this road, our baby would be with us.

* * *

Looking back, I sometimes wonder what Mama Jerono,[5] a mother from a nearby village, believed as she went into labor two years and nine months after my fateful trip to the hospital. It was not yet time for the baby inside of her to come when the cramping began on a warm evening in April.

She didn't have any bags packed, any plans to head to a hospital for the delivery. Instead, she lit a fire to make a plate of ugali for her hungry children. She tried to distract herself, to breathe the pain away as she stirred the maize flour into the pot of boiling water. It didn't work.

At least eight times before, Mama Jerono had done this work of laboring within her house mostly made from the earth.

But something was different this time around.

* * *

About halfway to the hospital, the rain for which we had been waiting began. At first, it was a mere drizzle, but then it poured from the night sky. The crops in the fields were thirsty. The farmers were desperate for the rain too.

Josh remarked under his breath, "No one told me it is freezing in Africa." While his complaint was serious, the car filled with laughter.

We approached a set of spikes laid out across the road. It was a police checkpoint, and Titus stepped out of the car to talk to the officer, explaining in Kalenjin that I was in labor. Well wishes for our growing family were passed, and we were on our way again.

By the time we reached the hospital, it was well after midnight.

---

5   In the Kalenjin culture, parents go by the name of their firstborn child.

The pale blue hallways echoed with the sounds of another mama screaming as she pushed to deliver her baby. Josh's eyes grew wide. He nervously laughed, "Oof! You did *not* prepare me for this." But when the screaming stopped, it was replaced by the beautiful sound of a newborn's cry.

Titus and Josh settled in the hallway while Allison and I entered a room marked: Laboring.

A single fluorescent light hummed and flickered from the center of the space. The walls matched the pale blue of the hallway. Two empty metal beds were waiting for whomever might come through the door. On the far side of the room was a doorway leading to a space designated for pushing and delivery. The smell of bleach filled the air.

The scene reminded me of the television show *Call the Midwife*—set in London in the 1950s—probably due to the combination of the well-starched nursing uniforms and the way the Kenyan medical system emulates the British.

The moment was especially 1950-esque when the nurse pushed one end of a cold metal horn into the bump of my belly while her ear rested on the other end listening for my baby's heartbeat. She assured me it was strong.

There was no electronic monitoring of the labor and delivery, nor was an epidural for controlling my pain one of the options for the day. I was given an oversized pink hospital gown that looked a lot like one of my Granny Reba's muumuu dresses.

I got seated on a large green exercise ball that I had insisted we carry to the hospital. I settled in, rocking back and forth, side to side, over and again, as I breathed in and out. It was the only somewhat-comfortable position I could find.

As the intensity of pain came and went, Allison sat quietly beside me, rubbing my back like I had done for her in the past. I rocked back and forth, side to side, breathing in and breathing out.

The metal bed next to mine functioned a lot like a revolving door for pregnant mamas who waddled into the space.

Some labored in silence while others were loud in their struggle. Like clockwork, within an hour of arriving, every other mama was ready to go through the doorway to push and deliver their baby. And when their work was finished, they walked back through the space with a baby in their arms. All the while, I rocked back and forth, side to side, breathing in and breathing out.

* * *

When the cramping came that night for Mama Jerono, it had only been a few months since the terrible day when her husband, the father of her children, had died in a freakish accident. A truck carrying gasoline crashed and exploded along the highway in Kipkaren. He was at the wrong place at the wrong time.

Trying to survive, Mama Jerono had numbed much of her sorrow, but now with her labor intensifying, the pain was overwhelming.

Mama Jerono lit a small kerosene lamp to light the room. Four of her children were already asleep in a row on the dirt floor. She laid down beside them and breathed in and out as the pain went from bad to worse to unbearable.

* * *

The night turned into morning, which led to afternoon and then to evening again. I was still rocking, walking, and trying to breathe.

Twenty-some hours after the contractions began, I was finally moved to the delivery room. I pushed and pushed with all the strength and determination I possessed, but my baby was stuck.

In nursing school, my professor explained that every woman gets to a point in labor where she's convinced she is going to die while trying to deliver her baby. As I breathed and pushed, I kept thinking, *I must be at that point she described, except what if I really am going to die? Mostly, I don't want my Ella to die. Oh, God!*

As I continued with this internal dialogue, my doctor calmly said, "Juli, I think we need to try a vacuum extraction."

"I don't think we want that, *daktari*," Allison nervously interjected. She wasn't a medical person, but her protective instincts understood that while it was intended for good, it was torturous.

But I was ready to be done. "If it will get my baby out, please do it."

After two failed attempts, my doctor leaned down again to listen to the heartbeat within my belly. His calm and reassuring tone changed as he emphatically said, "We need to do a C-section."

I simply nodded.

"Keep breathing," I said out loud, not caring who was listening or watching. Titus was by my side. His face told me he was afraid too.

All the other mamas had already left with their babies. Mine was still wedged inside of me. The path to the operating room—or the surgical theater, as it is known in Kenya—required going outside and through the rain.

Upon reaching a building that looked entirely like a warehouse, I realized we were at the OR. Titus wasn't allowed to go in with me, and we said good-bye.

My mind was slower than the hurry around me, taking in a final glance from Titus. I was writhing from the acute pain and afraid I might die—or worse—we could lose her. And now, I felt alone.

We had prayed for this baby. We had prepared for her coming, nesting, and rearranging oh-so-many parts of our lives to welcome her. As I waited impatiently for the C-section to begin, I reminded myself again to breathe, fighting for the life of our baby girl, Ella.

* * *

I awoke from anesthesia to a large surgical incision across my abdomen. Lights and flashing images slowly came together in patterns my mind could understand. My eyes remained closed. *I'm still alive.* Nurses wheeled me from the OR back outside on a gurney. I felt the sensation of rain on my face and each and every bump on the gravel path leading to a recovery room.

Titus was beside me. "*Tumbo inauma.*" My stomach hurts, I told him. The nurses kept pushing the gurney. My mouth would not stay quiet—I was coming off drugs and had no filter. Absolutely none. I knew what I was saying but could not stop.

Thank God I loved everyone in the hospital room and had nothing to clear up or get off my chest. I spoke of dancing robots and reiterated that drugs are indeed bad. I mentioned to Titus, "In the future, we should consider adoption as this day did not go particularly well."

In all my ramblings, my eyes stayed closed, but I kept asking, "Where's my baby? Where's Ella?"

I can still hear the sound of Allison's sweet voice, "She is right here beside you. And she's beautiful."

The day went differently than we had planned with one major exception: Ella and I were alive and well, making all the other traumas of the day seem insignificant. I was grateful, overwhelmingly so.

I knew in my mind and heart how very different the outcome could have been.

Shortly after meeting my tiny brown-eyed gift, my mind began to wonder about my neighbors, the mamas who labor and deliver in the community and don't have access to an emergency C-section when their crisis comes. By the time they know they need it, it is too late. I didn't feel guilty that Ella and I survived, but rather there was a sense of grief in the disparity that others do not always live.

* * *

I imagine Mama Jerono strained and pushed in silence until she could see the head of her baby, covered in black hair, crowning. She put her hands between her legs and continued in her labor, pushing the head and shoulders until she could pull the tiny baby's body into her arms.

Exhausted and relieved, she carefully tied string on the umbilical cord as her son let out a cry. Mama Jerono cut the cord with a razor blade and wrapped him in a blanket.

Her older girls, Rose and Sharon, woke up to the sound of their baby brother's crying. Mama Jerono asked them to walk to a neighbor's house to search for a cup of milk for her. The girls came back empty-handed.

Minutes later, with her baby still by her side, Mama Jerono passed out and her breathing stopped. Her girls watched on helplessly. Any emergency services their mama had needed were beyond their reach.

On the night Mama Jerono died, I was fast asleep in my bed a few miles away, unaware of the pain of a laboring and dying mama.

Unaware of the shift taking place within my universe.

3

Making Room

"I'm sorry if I'm broken." A tear escaped, telling of my sadness. Another month had gone by and there was still only one line on a stick.

"No, Juli," was all Titus said as he lovingly wrapped his arms around me, though he was disappointed too. We wanted a second child and were doing all we were supposed to on our part. Mapping out the right timing. Measuring lab tests that all looked fine. Waiting while feeling grateful for the child we already had. Waiting while aching for a brother or sister to come.

One night, in the quietest part of the night—somewhere in between when insects buzz and birds begin to sing—my mind was wide awake. Something changed within my prayers. I was asking for the same thing, but there was a shift, and I knew it.

I asked God to make room within our love and within our home for life to grow.

With the one exception of my post-labor chatter the night Ella was born, Titus and I had never talked about adopting a child. There was no earthly plan for what was about to unfold. I was simply praying for God to make enough space within me for new life.

* * *

I walked into Kimbilio Hospice like I have done many other times before over the past seven years. On this Friday afternoon, I stepped into the children's room, where the walls were covered with bright murals of animals. "Let everything that has breath praise the Lord"[6] is written above the window.

Joy, one of our long-term guests with cerebral palsy, lit up the room with her laughter when I entered it. "*Chamgei,* Joy," I greeted her, not lingering long as a premature baby wrapped in an oversized pink blanket had just arrived at the hospice. His mother's body, which had given him life and space to grow and develop, lay next door in the mortuary, being prepared for burial.

For the past five days, this premature infant had survived, against all odds, on water alone. His mother, Mama Jerono, had died in childbirth; his dad had been killed in a roadside accident. The baby was the youngest of eight brothers and sisters. A relative,

---

6   Psalm 150:6 NIV

I was told, had named him Ryan Kibichii, meaning *little king* and *survivor*.[7]

I held this baby wrapped in pink within my arms, and all I knew is that I wanted him to live. I called Laura —a pediatrician friend who lives in Eldoret— to discuss Ryan's case.

"Try to keep him warm, Juli," she said, "He can't autoregulate his temperature yet. Infection is very common for preemies. Feeding is most likely going to be a challenge."

Laura asked all the appropriate questions. "How far along was the mother in pregnancy? What happened to her? Prenatal care? HIV status?" She went on and on.

I did not have answers to any of these questions. *I do not know. I do not know. I do not know.*

Because of the many risks associated with Ryan's prematurity, she said to bring him in the following morning for review and, most likely, admission to the government hospital's neonatal intensive care unit. "One issue, though," she explained, "there is a hospital strike going on now in a neighboring county, so there are *lots* of babies here right now."

I hung up the phone and immediately called Titus. "Babe, there is this little baby here. The story is so sad. Can we take him

---

7   In the Kalenjin culture, a baby is given a name that represents the circumstances surrounding their birth. While they are still young, a child uses their first name and their Kalenjin name, which acts like a surname. In Ryan's family of eight children, they would all have different Kalenjin names.

   Once boys have gone through a rite of passage to become a man, they take on their father's Kalenjin name to be their surname. Girls typically take their husband's surname upon marriage.

   When I first visited Kenya, I was given a Kalenjin name to welcome me into the community. My Kalenjin name was Jepkios, the name given to a girl born too early. After I married Titus, I took on his surname of Boit.

   Nowadays, I am mostly referred to as Mama Ella, as parents go by the name of their firstborn child. But I am also called Bot Jerop, the mother of a girl born while it was raining.

to the hospital in Eldoret tomorrow morning?" Titus was used to this sort of phone call from me. He agreed as I went on to say words for which I didn't know the exact meaning: "Titus, I want to take care of this baby. I want him to live."

That was it. It wasn't about Ryan being a baby for me or for us. He wasn't sent to fill our void. Rather, I saw with clarity the worth and the vulnerability of this three-pound baby. I didn't need to be his savior, but I wanted to fight for him.

* * *

A social worker at Kimbilio Hospice contacted one of Ryan's relatives to accompany us to the hospital. In the early morning, I placed Ryan onto his auntie's bare chest and wrapped him there, hoping her warmth would be extended to his tiny frame.

The bright orange sun was rising from the east as Titus drove across the rugged terrain. We reached the pediatrician's office where she assessed Ryan and wrapped him back up in the pink blanket. Many questions were asked, and again, most of them had the same answer: "We don't know."

"Overall, he looks surprisingly good," the pediatrician said after a thorough review. "But I am concerned he needs more support for eating and staying warm. He needs some labs to rule out infection." She referred Ryan to be admitted to the NICU.

The space was overcrowded with miniature babies. Their mamas, still trying to heal from delivery, shuffled in at specific times to breastfeed or manually express the milk needed to help their baby grow. Mamas were required to wash their hands and put on hats and shoe covers before they could enter the room to see their babies for twenty minutes.

After the feeding session was complete, all the mamas had to leave. Nurses and doctors worked to maintain order and cleanliness, wanting to protect these fragile little ones who outnumbered them by a lot.

As much as I wanted to simply wash my hands and wear my hat and shoe covers like the other mamas, I was unable to blend in. Instead, I was known as "the *mzungu*," the white nurse from the hospice, and Ryan was referred to as "the unfortunate baby."

Two other premature babies shared Ryan's incubator with him. He slept nestled between them. I wondered about their stories. Their names. Their survival. *Were they able to communicate with one another in a language I was too big to understand? How much did they feel and sense?*

I started asking questions—lots and lots of questions. Some lived within my head while others were directed to the nurses and the pediatrician. *How long will Ryan need to be in the hospital? Is he tolerating his feeds? Gaining, or at least maintaining his weight? Does he have an infection? HIV? Are there signs of withdrawal?* Though I limited my texting and calls to once a day, I am sure the doctor wished she could block my phone number over the next twelve days.

More questions were wrestling within my spirit. *I wanted him desperately to live, but what happened if he did? Where would he go when he was discharged from the hospital?*

* * *

On the day Ryan first arrived at Kimbilio Hospice, Scott—one of Living Room's social workers and a neighbor of Ryan's family—briefed me, "He is the last-born of eight."

"Who is taking care of the other siblings?"

"After the burial tomorrow, they will basically take care of one another."

"Is there food for today?" I asked. Our team did this sort of work every day, but sometimes it was hard to know where to begin. In this situation, the children's loss was overwhelming. We had to start with the basics.

"Yes, but it will soon run out," Scott explained.

"Let's plan for a home visit on Monday. We'll do an assessment and come up with a plan for immediate help as we figure out long-term support."

That Monday, upon arriving at the children's simple home, our team greeted each of them with a handshake.

"*Habari yako?*" I asked. How are you?

Each child replied with the standard response, "*Nzuri.*" We are fine.

Seven brothers and sisters, with a few other neighborhood children interspersed, sat in a row on a wooden bench facing us. The landscape surrounding us was vast with beautiful shades of green and a bright blue sky. Chickens ate scraps off the dirt by our feet as a neighbor labored in his small field, using a hoe to break the hardened soil in preparation for planting maize.

My attention focused past the children's sweet faces onto the freshly dug grave just beyond them. It held their mother's body.[8]

Ten-year-old Sharon, while not the oldest, was bold in leading the introduction of her brothers and sisters. Light poured out from her sad eyes. "My name is Sharon," she spoke in Swahili, "and this is Jerono, Kiprotich, Moses, Rose, Alice, and Geoffrey." Their ages ranged from approximately three years old to eighteen.

---

8   In 2014, the first lady of Kenya, Mrs. Margaret Kenyatta, launched Beyond Zero, an initiative advocating for no woman to die while giving birth. Beyond Zero focuses on policy change, increased resource allocation, improved service delivery, and better individual health-seeking behaviors and practices.

An uncle who lived nearby mentioned that Alice, who was about eight years old, and Geoffrey, who was two or three, were often sick. "They cry and scream uncontrollably like something is hurting them. And Geoffrey's foot doesn't work so well."

"And Kiprotich's head is not right," another added. Some type of undiagnosed mental illness, he thought.

Jerono, the oldest sister, was living and working in Nairobi as a "house help," a maid of sorts, when she received the call that her mother had died. She hadn't known her mother was pregnant. Jerono came home to grieve and now was responsible for the care of her brothers and sisters. "I am asking myself: How will there be food?" she said. "I do not have an answer."

Sharon asked boldly, "How is baby Ryan?" She, along with the other younger siblings, was with their mother when she died. The weight of their loss, the trauma of it all, was gut-wrenching. They didn't speak of it as they were mostly trying to survive, but the grief was here. And it was heavy, weighing my heart down long after I left them. It was their little faces I thought of when I penned these lyrics.

> *What did your little eyes see?*
> *There were no tears today.*
> *What did your little eyes see?*
> *As your mama went away.*
>
> *What did your broken hearts feel?*
> *Were you too scared to say?*
> *What did your broken hearts feel?*
> *As your mama went away.*

Little eyes—I'll cry for you;
Though I don't know what to say.
Broken hearts—I'll fight for you.
Because your mama went away.

* * *

What does it look like to love in this situation? The question guided our team as we gathered to create a plan to help this family, mostly comprised of little people. Living Room's outreach team would schedule regular home visits to check in and reassess the situation. We would deliver basic food items weekly.

We decided that Moses, Rose, and Sharon would be enrolled in the boarding school in our community, which we hoped would create more stability and opportunity for them while reducing the workload for Jerono. We scheduled Geoffrey and Alice to be reviewed by a pediatrician and Kiprotich by a psychiatrist.

Clearly, the needs were many, and while the action steps made sense on paper, the complex reality, vulnerability, and pure grief of being orphaned was their new way of life. The freshly moved dirt covering their mama was a constant reminder of what they already knew through and through. They needed her, and she was gone.

* * *

"Titus, may Ryan come to our home when he is discharged from the hospital, at least until he's stable?" It was a big ask. Before he could reply, I went on, "The hospice isn't the right place for a premature baby. He needs hourly feedings with a clean, warm, and loving environment."

Titus was slow to respond, thinking deliberately through the implications both culturally as well as for our family. It was no small decision. I understood that.

Rightfully, Titus had concerns but, ultimately, he was willing for Ryan to come into our home. He scheduled a meeting with Ryan's extended family to explain our desire to help with his care. They agreed for him to come.

We were making decisions on behalf of a baby who still needed to be inside his mother's womb. He needed her warmth to protect him, her nutrients to feed him as his tummy was not ready to digest other foods. Ryan needed what his mama was no longer able to give.

We were making decisions on behalf of a baby whose parents were both buried in the red soil. There was much to grieve and process, but there was also a beautiful child who, against all odds, still had breath and life.

I wanted him to live. And so, as mamas do, I built a nest.

* * *

Much like the day Ella was born, dark clouds filled the sky and rain poured down as we left the hospital with Ryan asleep in an oversized car seat. A wooden rocking chair, protected by a tarp, was tied to the back of the truck, as if marking the moment in time. It wasn't telling us what might be ahead but simply the significance of today.

Most of what we were saying yes to was left unscripted. Something inside me knew: Everything we needed to learn would come from holding him, from listening to his heart, from watching him breathe. He would grow one breath at a time.

Ryan's life was not an accident and his story, as tragic as it felt, was far from over. His life was an invitation before us. What we were saying yes to was far from a full picture of what might come, no clear understanding of how long Ryan might be within our care or even be alive. Those were questions to be asked on other days.

Nothing or no one forced us one way or another. We had a choice, and it wasn't necessarily that there was a right or wrong way. But there was a yes and a no. There was a stopping to pay attention, interrupting our plans and the way we imagined our family would grow, as we chose to affirm Ryan's worth, to discern and discover—one day at a time—what it meant to love.

We were letting go of control in more ways than we understood in order to make room for life.

Some of it—perhaps most of it—we would only be able to see in retrospect and only because we chose to say yes.

* * *

"Ella, this is baby Ryan," I told our not yet three-year-old, uncertain of what I should be saying. "He's going to stay with us for a little while."

"This is my baby," Ella proudly announced, like Ryan was a puppy. I feared she might squish him, but Ella embraced Ryan with a love that helped lead Titus and me through all our hesitations and wonderings.

At home with Ella and baby Ryan

I fed Ryan each hour, drop by drop, praying the formula would stay down. My lofty and calculated goal was two teaspoons per feeding. Sometimes it worked.

Ryan slept almost non-stop in the early days, way more than Ella ever did in her first year of life, or so it felt. I held him close, rocking back and forth, the motion quieting both of us. I found myself whispering, "May joy be your strength, Ryan."

Laura—our pediatrician friend—sent a text offering a donation of frozen breast milk, letting me know that it was stored in the freezer of our friends, the Mamlins.

I texted Titus, "Babe, please stop by the Mamlins' home and pick up breast milk. Go with a bucket and ice."

My sweet husband didn't know what he had gotten himself into. He headed to the Coca-Cola factory in Eldoret to pick up a bucket of ice and proceeded to collect a few weeks' worth of liquid gold in the form of breast milk.

I giggled each time I opened the freezer to prepare a couple of spoonsful to feed Ryan. Our little black Kenyan baby was being fed Indian breast milk by a white American mama.

A global village was helping this boy to grow.

4

Protect the Rabbit

t was becoming night, and the newly acquired electricity was off again in our village. Our power supply isn't that reliable, and we are used to having intermittent outages that can last from hours to days. Titus stood beside me holding a flashlight as I changed Ryan's diaper.

It was one month since Ryan came to our home, and he was beginning to grow into his doll-sized preemie clothes. An hour had passed since his last feeding, and it was time for the next spoonful of formula before he went to sleep again.

"He doesn't need to leave," Titus quietly said.

"What?"

"He doesn't need to go anywhere."

"Okay," was all I needed to say for now.

It was an underwhelming declaration, and I knew it. A moment where a monumental decision was being announced, but we weren't ready for any more discussion or clarification. For a few more weeks, I sat with those words, pondering all they meant.

"Titus, what did you mean when you said Ryan doesn't need to leave?" I finally asked, ready for the next steps.

"We are going to raise Ryan." Once more, Titus declared what had already been established, "He does not need to leave."

Often, words from Titus' mouth would begin with the phrase, "Agui taught us…" Today was no different. His grandfather was a legendary figure in our region for his wisdom and wealth. He lived much of his early life as an orphan and outcast. Though I did not have the privilege of meeting Agui while he was alive, I have seen the impact of his reach for many miles around.

Agui's mother and grandmother were his primary caretakers, and both died when he was very young. At that time, in the early twentieth century, Kenya was still a colony of England, and formal education was seen by most Kenyans as being of little value. Missionary schools were often attended only by orphans and rejects of society, as was the case for Agui.

After completing basic education, Agui became a teacher and a planter of churches. He worked diligently and with amazing foresight. It also seems that everything he touched prospered.

Just before Kenya gained independence from Britain, Agui purchased land from the British government. While others rejected the absurdity of needing to buy their historic land from the settlers, Agui did it.

In 1963, Agui took a ten-year loan from the bank to purchase an expansive farm. At the time, the cost was equivalent to about one cent per acre. He paid it off in eleven years, and the farm has remained intact since, with Agui using a portion of the land to build a church and a high school that would become one of Kenya's foremost boys' schools.

On this day, as Titus and I navigated an unpredictable path, it was like Agui's guidance was leading his now-grown grandson in wisdom and the way of love.

"Agui told me a story about a rabbit being hunted by young boys on the farm. While they were chasing it, the rabbit ran into Agui's house for refuge. He was adamant that once it was under his roof, he needed to provide safety for the animal. I keep hearing Agui's voice talking about the rabbit when I think about what we should do in taking care of Ryan. We are to protect him."

"Okay, what does this mean exactly?" I asked knowing that in Kenya, family members typically step in unofficially to take care of a deceased relative's children. But we were not related to Ryan. What Titus was suggesting was beyond the cultural norm. "Should we do guardianship? Adoption? Who will be our attorney?"

Somewhat of a planner, I was looking for action items, preferably with accompanying timelines. A nice and neat process would be great. A few hundred other questions would follow. Almost none had answers yet.

* * *

During this time, Titus and I met with extended relatives of the children. They agreed that we would permanently care for Ryan as well as support his brothers and sisters.

The Living Room social work team followed up with Jerono and the children as planned. Geoffrey and Alice were reviewed by two pediatricians in Eldoret. Both ran tests. Neither gave a diagnosis.

One doctor mentioned that perhaps Alice suffered from psychological pain. "Come back," he said, "when they actually have the pain."

The explanation for Geoffrey's spastic right foot was thought to be a nerve injury in his leg from receiving a shot in his bottom, probably for malaria. Clearly, this was presumptive as we didn't know the details surrounding when it began, but it seemed to be a reasonable explanation.

We were told to try physical therapy and did so, but amid tremendous loss, there were many questions surrounding these little ones.

For Kiprotich, the psychiatrist gave him a diagnosis of schizophrenia, and like everywhere else in the world, managing his mental illness was full of challenges. Trying to ensure he took his medicine regularly. Adjusting doses because of side effects. Admitting him to the psych unit when it became too much. Protecting him and others from his vulnerabilities.

* * *

"We would like to apply to become guardians of a baby," Titus explained to the attorney. Titus shared more of Ryan's story, and the attorney wrote a list of documents we needed to collect and return to him.

I was listening, but my attention was distracted by the tall stack of legal files scattered around the room. They seemed haphazard, and I wondered if there was order to the clutter.

Weeks later, we returned with the necessary documents, and our case file was retrieved with ease. On the front of our file, in bold black marker, it read: BABY RYAN—ADOPTION CASE.

I half-smiled at Titus and breathed in a deep breath. A major decision seemed to have been made for us by what was written on a file folder, and, without looking back, we chose to proceed. This "Baby Ryan," whom we already loved and wanted, would officially and permanently become ours.

Or, at least, we hoped he would.

We quickly learned that working with our "adoption attorney" was a lot like the blind leading the blind. He acted confident in what he was advising us, but he did not seem to know the ABCs of Kenya's adoption laws.

A few months into the process, a friend directed us to an adoption agency to explore the process further. Their nearest branch was in Kisumu, a three-hour drive from our home.

We made the road trip and were warmly welcomed by a social worker for the agency. She showed us a large banner outlining the step-by-step process required in Kenyan adoptions—a much welcomed and overdue guide. Three reports needed to be submitted to the court in order to schedule an adoption hearing. Finally, we had a map to guide us.

"Your story does not fit neatly into the adoption agency categories," the social worker explained, "because Ryan did not come to you through a baby house. You were not prescreened. And you know extended family members, including Ryan's brothers and sisters."

All of this was true. We weren't planning to adopt a child. We wanted a baby but weren't expecting one to show up at Living Room's Kimbilio Hospice as a total orphan weighing three pounds, wrapped in a pink blanket. Ryan came into our care with no system or protocol in place to protect him and give him a chance to live. There were no services in place that provided formula, blankets, clothing, or diapers, not to mention willing hands who would hold him close, day and night, praying for him to live.

But our little king represented more than procedures and protocols, and I am grateful the social worker was able to recognize that. She interviewed Titus and me together, and then again separately. She asked questions about everything from our HIV status to why we would want to take care of someone else's child. She asked about my fertility patterns.

There were questions about my race being different than my husband's. Titus and I were to undergo counseling to wade through any mental health issues and were instructed to gather multiple supporting documents—including police clearance reports and bank statements with assets—proving we were caring people who would do our very best to love Ryan.

After our extensive meeting with the social worker, she scheduled a home visit the following week; she then sent us across the parking lot to meet with a counselor appointed by the adoption agency. It was a blistering hot afternoon in Kisumu, and the unpredictable electricity must have been off as we sat in a darkened ten by ten-foot room to meet with the counselor.

This man was tasked with assessing our psychological competency. He wasn't at all familiar with our situation, so he gave us a lot of information to prepare us mentally to receive a baby that was not our own. He went on and on, not leaving space for us to interject and explain that we already had the baby in our home. For nearly four months.

As he continued his discourse, I noticed Titus' head beginning to bop up and down, followed by the gentle sound of him snoring. I became anxious that the snoring would grow louder very soon. I tried to nudge Titus quietly to wake him up, and then, inappropriately, the crazy circumstances made me start to laugh. And the more I tried to stop, the harder it became to resist.

As serious questions were thrown at us about how we would cope with various scenarios that might come our way, I was mainly trying to keep Titus awake and myself from giggling.

Needless to say, I was a little concerned after the counseling appointment as to the report he might give. Even with our bad behavior, I hoped it was evident that we would wade through deep waters—even if imperfectly—to give Ryan a chance.

5

Squishy Baby Feet

Ryan was nearly six months old when, one night out of the blue, our easy-going baby started crying a cry I didn't recognize. It was one of pain but unlike any I had heard from him before. He was screaming relentlessly, and neither Titus nor I could make it go away.

"Maybe he's constipated," I suggested, trying to problem solve as the nurse and "pain expert" in our house. Ryan wasn't willing to put his feet down when we laid him on the bed. Something about being flat seemed to aggravate the pain.

In the dark of this night, Titus said, "Juli, something is wrong with Ryan's feet. They are swollen, and they hurt."

"Titus, he has squishy baby feet. How do you know they're swollen? And why would his feet hurt?"

Titus was right, of course, but I wasn't ready to comprehend why. I called Laura the next day and explained, "It's weird but something is going on with Ryan's feet."

Laura asked questions about Ryan's family history to which I still didn't know any of the answers. Then she said, "None of the siblings have sickle cell disease, right?"

"I don't think so. Wouldn't we know by now?"

"It's highly unlikely Ryan has it," she explained, "if none of the other seven siblings do, but bring him for review tomorrow. We'll do some tests to see what's going on."

When Laura mentioned sickle cell disease, I was immediately transported to my early days as a nurse when I worked in Los Angeles and often took care of "sicklers," as we called them.

Young adults—mostly African American—roamed the hallways stooped over and crippled by pain, hanging on to their IV poles. We tried to help break the crisis of pain by pumping fluids and narcotics through their veins.

One of my patients, a woman of twenty, tried to put words to her pain. "You know how much it hurts when you stub your toe and the pain shoots up your foot and leg?" she asked me. "It's that type of sensation times a million. And it doesn't go away."

I never forgot the intensity in her eyes as she described the experience, nor how sad I felt when she died from complications of her disease just a few days later.

Another patient came to mind whom I took care of fifteen years ago, but the memory of his suffering felt like it happened yesterday. He was a kind and shy young man with priapism, a common and excruciatingly painful condition associated with sickle cell that causes prolonged erection. His lasted for several days. He couldn't wear clothes or cover himself as it hurt too much. He apologized with embarrassment each time I entered the room.

Oh God, please don't let it be this.

The next afternoon, we drove to Laura's home where she carefully reviewed our sweet Ryan and sent us to the lab for some tests. The results took a week to get back. As we waited, the pain in Ryan's feet eased, but the worry heightened in me as I began to read about the horror of sickle cell disease—especially here in Kenya.

The numbers knocked the wind out of me. Was it true that every day a thousand children are born in Sub-Saharan Africa with this disease? And even more crushing, that fifty percent of them died before they turned two? And up to ninety percent by the age of five?

Would this be Ryan's story?

The pathology results came by email. A PDF held the expected but devastating news that Ryan had sickle cell disease.[9] Countless times over the years, I have sat with parents and shared news that no one ever wants to hear. Now it was my turn. I knew all the other siblings had to be tested too, but for today, I was going to focus on Ryan and grieve.

"Can you come home?" Tears streamed down my face. "He has it." While these words had less context for Titus, he understood well. He, too, had watched friends suffer and die from this awful disease.

---

9   Sickle cell disease (SCD) is an inherited red blood cell disorder. In someone who has SCD, instead of having round red blood cells that carry oxygen to all parts of the body, some of their red blood cells are C-shaped, like a sickle.

These cells also become hard and sticky, so when they travel through small blood vessels, they get stuck and clog the blood flow. This causes pain and other serious life-threatening problems.

All because of a single error in Ryan's DNA code, a T that should have been an A.

I stepped outside to take some deep breaths. Everything hurt. The afternoon sun was warm and shining brightly on my face. A pair of turacos were singing loudly in the trees above and then majestically flew overhead, flaunting their beautiful red wings. The words of Jesus flooded my mind: If I take care of the birds, I will take care of you.

Oh, how I wanted to fix what was unfixable, to rewind the clock to something a little simpler. I couldn't comprehend how much Ryan's body ached, or how much he would suffer in the days ahead. Yet I felt the heaviness of his disease combined with how dramatically his prognosis was affected by where we live.

In the US, the life expectancy for a person living with sickle cell disease was forty-two years; and while that isn't good, it was very different than the two-year life expectancy in Kenya. My mind reeled as my heart raced—this was too much. *I don't want this.*

I repeated these words to my parents who were a world away, "I don't want this for Ryan, or for us." They were quiet as I processed and grieved. "I don't want this for anyone. Why are the kids here dying before they turn two? Why are there such better outcomes for them in other places?"

* * *

Titus and a social worker from Living Room took Ryan's brothers and sisters for sickle cell screening tests at the government hospital in Eldoret. The results for this test came back the same day.

I was working at the hospice when I saw a text from Titus, "Tears have fallen today," he wrote. I didn't need to read any further but continued, "Geoffrey and Alice have sickle cell too. The rest have the trait."[10]

"Lord, I don't want this," I whispered. These kids had already suffered too much. Alice and Geoffrey had, by now, outlived their life expectancy. Their episodes of pain and Geoffrey's spastic foot finally made sense.

All I replied was, "*Pole,* Titus." I am sorry.

* * *

Nothing prepares a parent for the moment they must walk into a cancer center with their child as a patient—or in our case, three children on the same day. Countless times I entered this building as a nurse practitioner to provide other patients and families palliative care.

On this Tuesday morning, my role changed. I entered as a mother. Defensive and heartbroken, trying not to completely melt down, I was living what felt like a nightmare. I did not imagine this story would be mine. Tears filled my eyes as I scanned the sea of faces, mostly women and children coming for the clinic.

Today's outpatient services were geared for children with various cancers and blood diseases. The look in the other mamas' eyes told me I was not alone, but the sense of solidarity I felt was not reassuring. At least not today.

So many of their stories, I knew, were filled with untold struggle. I now joined the mamas wanting their babies to live. Mamas hoping for relief from the pain without easy access to care.

---

10 People who have sickle cell trait inherit one sickle cell gene from one parent and one normal gene from the other parent. Those with the trait usually don't have any signs of the disease, but they can pass the trait on to their children. And if their partner also has sickle cell trait, there is a 25% chance that any child of theirs will have sickle cell disease.

Long lines of people with no clear direction as to where we should go next created a sense of chaos all around.

The young lady behind the reception desk was scrolling on her phone. There was no, "How may I help you?" No, "Please have a seat, I will be right with you." She didn't look up with any sense of concern that my children or I had a name and a story that mattered in her world.

Perhaps she was as overwhelmed as the rest of us by the suffering, and her defense mechanisms were getting the best of her too.

I wondered if the other moms were having the same internal dialogue I was having, but I supposed they had become accustomed to being treated this way. Their prayers were undoubtedly much like mine: I wanted Ryan and his siblings to survive, no matter the cost. I was humbly aware, though—as horrible as it was that the children were sick with a devastating disease—the ones I cared for had an unfair advantage.

I felt the burden of Ryan, Geoffrey, and Alice's disease deeply, but I also recognized that I had resources to navigate the daunting system.

I had fifteen years of nursing experience and a wealth of community support and connections—both locally and beyond—people who were ready and willing to assist our family. We weren't living on a dollar a day and making impossible choices that affected our children's treatment and, ultimately, their survival outcome. And I hadn't walked miles, nor had I traveled hours by public transportation to reach the hospital.

I woke up with my grief, got the children ready, and drove by car.

As I sat waiting to pick up lab results, the hematologist, a friend of mine, came and asked why I was sitting in line. He knew that as a clinician, I was allowed to skip the lines.

"Sometimes, it's important to wait," I told him.

We entered the consultation room, and the doctor asked a series of questions. Some I could answer and others, once again, I could not. One by one, Ryan, Geoffrey, and Alice were assessed. Important medicines like penicillin were prescribed to protect their small bodies from bacterial diseases for which they were at high risk.

We left with the instructions to watch for a fever—all fevers are an emergency in sickle cell patients. "The pain crises," the doctor said, "are unpredictable. Avoid triggers like dehydration, illnesses, high altitude, and cold temperatures."

While I could do my best to keep them hydrated, we live at six thousand feet, and as their Uncle Mosh would attest, it gets cold sometimes, even if we live on the equator.

The doctor could offer no hotline phone number for the night the unrelenting pain would return. Thankfully, I had phone numbers of several pediatricians I could call for help. And when the pain proved to be unbearable, I had access to morphine through the hospice.

What did the other mamas do? I wondered, thinking of the long line of those still waiting outside. What do they do when the pain is too much? When the fever comes in the night and there isn't a car to drive to the hospital? What do they do when the screaming won't stop, and they feel gutted by their helplessness?

I felt this weight while still having connections and resources.

One final word of warning from the doctor gripped our hearts before we were sent out to fend on our own: "Be aware," he said, "over time, sickle cell disease can be harmful to a patient's spleen, brain, eyes, lungs, liver, heart, kidneys, penis, joints, bones, or skin."

And on this alarming note, we were told to come back in a month for review.

***

Two years earlier, I stood on a bustling street corner in Eldoret to meet up with my friend Abi, who was getting ready to move back to America with her family. It was 2014, and Ella was a baby. Abi had a few household items and baby gear she wanted to pass on to me.

We hugged one another as street vendors were selling their daily wares all around. We were participants in the normal buzz and congestion of pedestrians walking, motorbikes ferrying passengers, and cars driving in all directions.

I was familiar with bits and pieces of Abi's story, but mostly from a distance. She and her husband were wrapping up their work in a pediatric HIV program as they had recently become guardians of twin boys with sickle cell disease. Because of the complexity of their illness, Jordan and Abi were moving the twins to America for treatment.

I don't remember the specific words Abi spoke that day, but the degree of love I saw in her eyes was etched in my heart. I could not have known then that I would one day share much of that same love.

When we received Ryan's diagnosis, I reached out to Abi immediately by email. I had many questions, and I needed a friend who understood the mountain Titus and I faced. I was learning what my combined role of nurse practitioner, advocate, and mom needed to involve. Searching far and wide for answers. Learning the questions that needed to be explored.

I asked Abi about the standards of care in the US that led to such drastically different outcomes. What resources were available within Kenya? Practically, what did my baby need to survive? What could I do to help Ryan live to reach age two? Or five?

Adulthood? And what could be done to help him not only *survive* but possibly *thrive*?

Abi's response was kind and loving. She updated me on their journey and shared how their twins had undergone bone marrow transplants, the only option of a cure for sickle cell disease. I reread her words a few times as I was not aware this was even a possibility. For them, a transplant led to their one son being free from sickle cell while the other transplant failed due to complications.

Though a transplant seemed like an impossibility, a small seed of hope took root within me. Abi included a YouTube link to a song. In the still of the night, I clicked it. I was sitting in our bed, my mind wide awake while Titus slept beside me.

Surprisingly, our internet was functioning at a speed that allowed the video to open and play. I don't know who first penned the words, "Music is what feelings sound like," but my grief broke open as the first chord was played. These lyrics followed like a salve for my soul.[11]

There is strength within the sorrow, there is beauty in our tears
You meet us in our mourning, with a love that casts out fear
You are working in our waiting, sanctifying us
When beyond our understanding, you're teaching us to trust
Your plans are still to prosper, you have not forgotten us
You're with us in the fire and the flood
Faithful forever, perfect in love
You are sovereign over us

---

11 "Sovereign Over Us" by Aaron Keyes, Jack Mooring, and Bryan Brown. Used by permission.

6

Afraid of the Pain

sat on the tile floor of our living room next to Ryan, mesmerized by his play. He scooted on his belly, absent of pain, laughing freely. It had been weeks since I last heard him laugh. I looked into Ryan's eyes and felt a little like the boy in the movie *Hook*, in the scene where he didn't believe the man in front of him was Peter Pan. He stared long and hard, rubbing his face until he eventually had eyes to see it was really him. Ryan was back.

"There you are," I whispered under my breath, realizing how much I missed our baby. Ryan's personality was overshadowed by pain that swallowed up his ability to engage, laugh, and play. But here he was, even if only for a few moments. I took it all in.

Ella couldn't see Ryan's owies with her eyes, but she knew when they were around. His crying reliably let us know how much it hurt. I was challenged with explaining to her how to play with her baby brother.

"Don't touch Ryan's hands, Ella. They hurt today."

"Careful, Ella, don't touch his feet. They have owies."

"Oh Ella, don't pick him up. Ryan's hurting."

I wrestled with the tension of wanting Ella and Ryan to bond and play together as they should, while also being uncertain of how to protect them both from his pain.

Titus and I were having more conversations about a bigger picture, including all of Ryan's siblings. It wasn't particularly well thought out, but at breakfast one morning, Titus casually said, "I don't want Ryan to grow up and ask why we didn't help his brothers and sisters."

These words were spoken in a very similar fashion and tone to Titus' announcement that Ryan didn't need to go anywhere. Once again, we didn't try to clarify in the moment. The love we held for Ryan, unbeknownst to him, was guiding our family on many levels.

At first, it wasn't simply about loving or including the other siblings, but more about how our care—or lack thereof—might affect Ryan. While there were layers in place to support the brothers and sisters, they were further outside the walls of our home.

Slowly, those clear divisions began to blur.

* * *

Much was happening in our world. We were in a waiting pattern for adoption proceedings to be completed and potential treatment options for the kids to come together, but long lists of decisions had to be navigated each day.

I didn't know how to process all of it myself, let alone know how to best parent Ella's strong and tender heart along the way. I wanted there to be enough space for her to learn about kindness and love, to feel safe and protected. I wanted it to occur in a more controlled sort of way than we had available. I wanted it to be easier, less messy, with less suffering. I wanted there to be fewer opportunities for her and the rest of us to get hurt along the way.

One conclusion I came to was that I would fight for Ryan and his siblings in the same way I would want any other mama to fight for Ella were she in the same situation. I would fight with all the imperfect love my heart contained and a never-give-up grit I felt down in my core.

In spite of my determination, I was in fear of Ryan's pain, of where it might lead us. This fear also extended to Alice and Geoffrey, but at this point, my protective heart kept them at a safe distance as Ryan's siblings, *not* my kids. I didn't want the chronic pain or the eventual death to steal Ryan from us, and I was wrestling with the grief of it all.

I met with a counselor visiting from the US to talk through some of the angst I was experiencing. In a lengthy session, we did memory work where I was guided to envision something that wasn't a memory from the past but rather something like a dream of the future. The scene was vivid in my mind's eye, unlike anything I had ever experienced.

I imagined three kids in light blue hospital pajamas. We were in a US hospital, and the children were crying, as they were experiencing much pain and suffering. I could not see their faces, but I knew them to be Ryan, Geoffrey, and Alice. Most clear to me was the assurance that their suffering was leading toward healing and life instead of death.

Long after the counseling session ended, those images stayed with me. Not as a promise so much as a guide. We were to go after their healing, even if it seemed impossible.

* * *

Around this time, I emailed back and forth with my friend Jodi, a pediatric transplant doctor in Indiana. She wrote, "Juli, I highly encourage you to have the kids tested to see if any of the siblings might be a match. We are having good outcomes with almost a hundred percent cure rate for children with sickle cell who have a matched sibling donor."

I began to call around and do my homework to see how to get the HLA testing[12] done. This process was critical for identifying if any of the siblings could safely donate their bone marrow to Ryan, Geoffrey, or Alice.

My findings were discouraging. No laboratories near us were able to do the cheek swabs to send out for testing. But even if they could do the swabs, not a single lab in Kenya was able to run the tests since a bone marrow transplant was not available within the country or even the larger region.

I remembered a case two years prior, in which we had helped a boy from our community go to India for a bone marrow transplant. I reached out to the caseworker who had assisted with the travel, explaining our current situation. Her company did not

---

12 Human leukocyte antigen (HLA) typing is used to match patients and donors
    for a bone marrow transplant. HLA are proteins—or markers—found on most
    cells in your body. Your immune system uses these markers to recognize which
    cells belong in your body and which do not. HLA matching is based on 10 HLA
    markers. The more markers two people share, the better the match.

send patients to the US for treatment, but I asked if she could help me coordinate the process of screening and sending the swabs to a lab in New York for testing.

After days of figuring out all the logistics, a long line of siblings sat in a row in a doctor's office in Eldoret. It was Valentine's Day. Lots of cheek swabs were done. Even with the explanations given, confused looks filled the kids' faces as they tried to imagine what we were doing.

Medical forms were filled out, cross-checked and signed. The cost to know if there might be a cure possible for these children? $684. Each sibling had a twenty-five percent chance of being an identical, 10/10 match for Ryan, Geoffrey, and Alice.

As we waited for the results—it took about a month—I didn't allow myself to do any further research or planning related to transplants. Titus and I didn't talk through the what-ifs, and I did an unusually good job of not letting my thoughts be consumed by what may come. We simply waited and prayed.

I desperately wanted the kids to have the chance to be freed from the disease, but the results were not something I could manipulate or control.

* * *

It was a Saturday night in March when the emails came. The first message from the caseworker arrived at 8:48 p.m. and read, "I am awaiting results for Ryan and Alice. Please find results for Geoffrey Kiplagat matching with Sharon Chepkorir: 10/10 match."

At 9:39 p.m., the second message came. "Alice Jepkirui: No match. Ryan Kibichii: Full match with Sharon Chepkorir. 10/10."

The waiting was over. The news bittersweet. As our hematologist later described, Geoffrey and Ryan got a golden ticket while Alice did not.

On this night, there wasn't much heart space for me to wrestle through the questions—science-based, existential, or otherwise. Why for Geoffrey and Ryan and not for Alice? It wasn't that I didn't feel the weight of it—it was simply too much.

Titus and I decided to wait to share the results with the children until the information held practical meaning to them.

I forwarded the reports to Dr. Jodi the next day and asked for input and possible next steps. I was certain there were at least 1,001 to be taken. From the other side of the globe, Titus and I talked to Jodi by phone. She walked us through transplant procedures, risks, and her recommendations. Her knowledge, experience, and kindness led us down a path that seemed both hard and right.

One comment Jodi said stood out to me the most, "To get through transplant, you need community support. It's the only way to make it."

I knew what Jodi was describing when she talked about community—we lived it within our village. Neighbors caring deeply about one another in vibrant, rich, and practical everyday sort of ways. And our work at Kimbilio is nothing but a beautiful picture of the gift of community.

Titus and I began to talk through our questions and concerns about where to go and what we hoped we would still be able to offer our children. Very early on, Titus said, "I want my sister to go with us. Linda could help with the kids."

Our children knew and loved their Auntie Linda, whom we simply referred to as Senge, Kalenjin for *aunt*. She was kind and reliable and would be a piece of home—if given the opportunity.

There were many other details to sort through, but her coming was always a part of the ongoing conversation.

* * *

I never met Mama Jerono, but I often dream of who she was. I imagine her through the lens of her remarkable children. The sound of her laughter. What she liked. The struggles she faced. The hopes that caused her to get up each day and do life, one more time.

Much of who I am is shaped by the patients I've cared for over the years in Kenya. When I think of Mama Jerono, I see faces like that of Maggie, a thirty-something-year-old mother of five who came to Kimbilio Hospice to spend her final months of life.

As a new mama myself, I was privileged to sit at Maggie's side and navigate the hard path of cancer and dying, to let her tears mingle with mine as she hugged me tightly with her remaining arm. Her only request: "Please make sure my children are okay."

Love had led her to ask that of me, and it helped me to listen. To slow down and pay attention, to let the weight of her words sink in deep.

I'm often guided by Maggie's voice, from one mother to another, as I look at Ryan and his brothers and sisters. I imagine their mama would say the same: "Please make sure my children are okay." But on many days, Mama Jerono's children were not okay. As we explored possible treatment centers for Ryan and Geoffrey, Alice became sick.

On a Friday morning in May, Alice developed a high fever, excruciating pain in her belly, and shortness of breath. Titus and I rushed her to Eldoret. She laid across my lap in the backseat, making gasping sounds. I felt helpless and afraid.

The police stopped our car as Titus tried to rush his way through town, but with one look at Alice's condition, the policeman sent us back on our way.

The laboratory results showed malaria and a hemoglobin of five, less than half of the blood supply she needed. Her breathing was labored. Alice was admitted to the pediatric ward for treatment, and to get her blood with countrywide shortages, Titus and his cousins went to give theirs.

Within forty-eight hours, Geoffrey was in the same condition, only worse. He developed acute chest syndrome, a complication of sickle cell disease requiring intensive care. A face mask supplied oxygen to his tired body. He was afraid and cried when the nurses needed to give him medication.

Geoffrey was in pain, so I asked the pediatrician—a friend of mine—what he was going to do about it.

"Geoffrey needs morphine," he said.

"Then please give it to him."

"There isn't any currently in the hospital." No matter how good the doctors in Kenya are, they are often under-resourced.

"May I supply morphine for Geoffrey from the hospice?" Thankfully, my crazy request was granted. *But what about the other children whose mamas didn't run a hospice, who didn't have access to morphine? What happened to them when their pain crisis came?*

As overwhelmed as I was by my child's suffering, years of noticing the pain of others, of advocating for the poor didn't stop simply because it had become my personal story. With every step, I wrestled with the disparities that were all around.

* * *

After ten days, Alice was ready to be discharged. Geoffrey, on the other hand, was struggling for every single breath. Alice told her little brother, "Bye, Geoffrey. *Utapona.*" You will be healed. There was such tenderness in her small voice, followed by his tears as she headed home.

But where was home? Where would she go to recover? The decision was made that for now, our home was the best option. Titus held Alice's hand and led her down the stairs from the pediatric ward to the car—a moment capturing Titus' unusual capacity to couple kindness and strength.

It didn't strike me until much later that Alice left the hospital with only the clothes on her back and a black plastic bag filled with four oranges. No change of clothes. Not even a toothbrush.

When we reached home, a makeshift bed was prepared. Alice ate her supper, took a slew of medicines, and slept in a Kimbilio T-shirt of mine.

As I tucked her into bed, I imagined what it must feel like for her, an eight-year-old child, to be in another new place. I hoped that like the word plastered across the shirt, our home would be a refuge for her.

Weeks later, Geoffrey followed Alice to our home. He wasn't better yet as his fevers were still uncontrollable, a dangerous sign for little ones with sickle cell disease. It was a bold move for the doctors to discharge him, but they had reached the limits of what they could do. Geoffrey came home, and we did our best to provide for his physical and emotional needs.

Our home was an eight hundred square foot, two-bedroom house. For our neighborhood, that is spacious. Ryan slept in our room and Ella was happy to have the other children come for a sleepover. She was three years old and welcoming but also clearly in charge of her toys and space. On an early morning, just as the birds started to announce a new day, I sat in our living room trying to make sense of the place we had reached. Ella was awake beside me, all wrapped up in a cozy blanket.

"Mama, where did we get all these kids?" She was referring to Alice and Geoffrey as Ryan was her baby, remember?

"Ella, their mama and baba died." I was unsure of what to say. "They are sick and need a place to stay."

"Are we going to keep them?" she wondered innocently.

"I don't know, Ella. Would that be alright with you?"

"It's okay," she said sweetly. And that was it. At least for now. Ella began to play, carrying on with her day with a simple innocence I longed for.

7

Making a Map

created a map on a scrap of paper. It was done in pencil, by hand. The map looked more like an algorithm I would use at the hospice to treat nausea or hiccups.

Give treatment A. If it works, continue with treatment A. If not, increase dose of treatment A, add treatment B or switch to treatment C.

I put the lists floating in my head into a flowchart, trying to solve for the many variables beyond my control, organizing on paper all that needed to happen to reach a single goal: to travel with the children to the US to get the care they needed.

The adoption and guardianship process were significant variables within that flowchart, requiring specific reports from various governmental agencies before a judge could rule in our favor.

And until such a ruling, we could not apply for Kenyan passports for the children. We could neither apply for US visas, nor could we add the children to our health insurance.

There were decisions about where to go for treatment, but those were contingent on all the other pieces coming together. *Where would we live? What needed to be arranged for us to indefinitely leave our work and home in Kenya? Would we need a car in the US? Could Senge go with us to help care for all our kids?*

I wrote it all on my chart, not knowing how it would end up or what we were really signing up for. There wasn't extraordinary faith or ability on my part, but my soul demanded we keep trying—one wobbly step at a time—because these children were worth every step.

* * *

The banner at the adoption agency had outlined the step-by-step process required in Kenyan adoptions. Two favorable reports had already been submitted to the court. To proceed with the adoption hearing, we still needed the third.

"Once the adoption agency reports are filed, come back, then we will submit ours," someone from this office had said to Titus and me.

As instructed, we were back. We entered the office of a man I'll call Mr. John. He swung back and forth in his leather office chair, his demeanor and mannerisms shouting that he was in charge. On the wall behind him, a piece of paper was taped and read something to the effect of, "If your best isn't good enough, that isn't my problem. You will have to deal with it."

"I cannot give you a favorable report," Mr. John began bluntly. "I won't do it." His voice escalated toward yelling, catching me off guard. "You haven't followed the right procedures. Who knows, she might traffic the child."

The *she* referred to *me*.

It was hard to make sense of his words. There was no rhyme, reason, or evidence as to what he was asserting. While he was unable to see our motives, our actions were reflecting the very thing he said was his job to do.

We were fighting to protect Ryan, giving him a home and family. There was nothing illegal or immoral about us doing it. Kenyan law allowed for us to adopt because of Titus' Kenyan citizenship. And Mr. John knew this.

Questions flooded my spinning head. *Was he really going to block the adoption? Was this his way of asking for a bribe? Was something else at work here?* I didn't understand what was happening.

Calm as always, Titus replied, "The other reports have already been submitted to the court. We are hoping to finish the adoption as soon as possible so we can continue the medical treatment Ryan and his siblings need. Kenya is our home," Titus continued. "My wife has lived in Kenya for twelve years. We have our home, child, work, and family here. We are not going to traffic Ryan."

Titus handed over medical records and letters of support from Ryan's doctors. The officer read them and said, "I don't believe these letters. How am I supposed to know these are real doctors?"

"Do you want to meet them?" I asked.

Mr. John looked at me. "What happens to other children who have this condition in Kenya?"

"Mostly, they die," I replied. "Up to ninety percent by the age of five." There was no other answer to give.

His chair continued to swing around. "Well, doesn't it say somewhere in the Bible," he paused, "to die is gain?"

My face was instantly hot and red in a mixture of sadness and anger. I could not imagine any words more vulgar or offensive than what he just said.

I don't remember deciding to stand up; it was like an involuntary reflex. I turned to Titus. "I'm sorry," I whispered, "I can't do this."

My kind husband was hurt too, but he knew he had to stay to fight on behalf of our little ones.

As I headed for the door, Mr. John asked me to sit back down, but the mama bear within me had been poked. She was not going to be easily quieted.

I am pretty sure he felt as if he had won. But for the sake of whom? And why? We needed his recommendation to move ahead with the adoption, and it seemed unlikely, at best, that he was going to give it.

With bitter tears in my eyes and a fire lit in my belly, I looked at him and quietly said, "You're wrong. It is not better for them to die when we have the opportunity to fight for them to live. You have the power to help make it possible. Don't tell me it's better for them to die. And *don't* misuse the Bible."

Tears flowed in streams down my face as I closed the door behind me. They weren't likely to stop for a while.

* * *

A few days later, Mr. John came for a home visit. My stomach was in knots thinking about our previous meeting. I hoped seeing Ryan and Geoffrey in our home would put names and faces to the story we were telling.

As Mr. John entered our house, he saw Ryan and announced, "The child doesn't look sick to me. Let me see his medicine."

Such a dangerous combination of ignorance and arrogance. I clenched my teeth to hold in the words I wanted to say. They wouldn't help Ryan. I brought the large box of medications and set them in front of him.

A series of questions followed and then suddenly, without warning, Mr. John stood up and walked out of the house.

There was no thank you. No good-bye. He simply left.

* * *

Mr. John phoned Titus days later, asking us to return to his office. We braced ourselves for impact as we waited in line on the wooden bench in the hallway.

Blunt as always, Mr. John told us, "When I visited your home, I was moved with compassion and decided to write a report in support of the child's adoption. However, now that I've had time to think about it, I know compassion cannot be my guide. I will not be writing a supporting document."

We knew by this point that there was no use in trying to convince this man of anything. Titus and I left the office in silence.

We had prayed for months for favor in this journey. We asked God to protect Ryan, to make a way for his adoption to go through and for him to get treatment. We worked incessantly toward these goals. And now, one man—a man who refused to be guided by compassion—stood in our way.

Ten minutes later, while Titus and I were still sitting in the car in silence, unsure of what to do next, Mr. John called. He told Titus that one of his superiors called him regarding the case, and he would write the report for us after all.

"What? Are you serious?" I told Titus. I was exhausted from all the whiplash. "Who called him?"

"I don't know," Titus said. "Maybe it was Jesus." We laughed, exhaling in the momentary relief. We knew this specific report would only assist Ryan. We still needed to go back on behalf of Geoffrey and Sharon to fight for their guardianship too.

But for now, we thanked Jesus for a much-needed miracle.

8

Community

"You need community to get through transplant," Jodi's words remained in my head as a friend of mine, a former transplant doctor from Indiana University, came for a visit to Kimbilio. We stood in the hallway of the hospice, life and death happening all around, and talked about what treatment could be like for my kids.

"We are looking at coming to Indianapolis for the boys' transplants," I said, "but I am wondering what options might be available for Alice."

My friend patiently listened to me. "Juli, I want to connect you with a good friend of mine at UCLA who is working on a study using gene therapy to treat sickle cell," he said. "It might be an option one day for Alice."

A few days later, I received an email from my friend that led to a series of conversations and introductions with the transplant team at UCLA. It was clear that gene therapy was not yet an option for Alice, but research studies were beginning that hopefully would lead to treatment possibilities for her someday.

One of the introductions was with Dr. Moore, the head of the pediatric bone marrow transplant program at UCLA. After weeks of emailing back and forth, a phone call was set up. It was morning in Los Angeles and a busy workday for Dr. Moore. In the same way Dr. Jodi was generous with her valuable time, Dr. Moore talked to me from the other side of the world with kindness and warmth I will never forget. For nearly forty-five minutes, he talked about the risks and benefits of doing a transplant.

"The days and weeks after transplant require much patience as healing is a slow process," he said. "There is great risk for infection—even a simple cold can kill these kids in the initial days as they have no immune system to fight it."

All the information was important and welcome, yet daunting. At this point, the data had no personal context, nor could I begin to grasp the meaning of some of what was being shared. Thankfully, I could not fathom how hard it might get. I could only hope that my kids would get the chance to be freed from this cruel disease.

The following day, Dr. Moore emailed this message, "We are called to minister to folks through some very tough times, and that is what we want to do. Unfortunately, none of these processes are benign, and they carry significant life-threatening risks with them along with the hope for a cure. That makes the decision-making process very difficult.

"We want to help inform you about the process as much as possible, provide our recommendations, and then help assist you and your husband in your decision-making process. I like to think of my patients as if they were my children and what I would do for them before making any recommendation.

"Prayers for wisdom are the most important so that God grants wisdom to you and your husband and the correct direction. Please feel free to email me at any time."

Dr. Moore's message, along with Jodi's wise words, led us to decide that if we were given the opportunity to do transplants, Los Angeles would be our choice and UCLA would be our treatment center. While the idea of the boys "getting the chance" still seemed like an outlandish and impossible feat, the truth was that I was getting used to watching God do the impossible.

* * *

Over the years, as I stepped closer to those in their suffering, I came to recognize the nearness of God—present in the hard places and the pain, in the spaces where death and destruction always wanted to win. Faith expressing itself as love in its purest, most sacrificial form made room for miracles to come. Most of them, not quickly.

Sometimes, God's presence came through a meal prepared and served, one bite at a time. Each morsel or sip requiring untold effort, a symbol of love. Through baths given with kindness, dignity was restored. In the cleaning of wounds, putrid from neglect, or in the singing of hope-filled words, even when they were impossible to feel, God's nearness was palpable.

Much of my life's work could be summed up in a willingness to do what others think cannot be done, attempting hard things with no promise of what the outcome might be.

Like the time I fought for a malnourished orphan from our community named Flovia, wanting her to live while not being sure if she would survive. Or when I wanted comfort for Maggie, for her kids to be cared for—not sure what it would look like but being willing to try.

It often involved simply saying yes to what was before me. There was no assurance of success but more often a guiding question: *What does it look like to love in this situation?*

Years of practice had given me the courage to try again. To love again. To hope again. The grit and resilience required for this journey developed little by little, one yes at a time.

In the same way the Bible speaks of the God of Abraham, Isaac, and Jacob from long ago, David Tarus talks of the God of Flovia today. At two years old, Flovia was on the verge of death. But the God of Flovia put love within us to simply try, and *that* God restored her life, giving her a chance to grow and us a glimpse into the work of love for which we were made.

That same God who rescued Flovia gave us hope to keep trying, making way for story upon story. Now, we were calling on the God of Ryan, Geoffrey, and Alice to once more bend down low and listen to our prayers.

History did not allow me to give up too easily on love. I held onto it as we searched high and low for where our kids might receive treatment. As we selected an insurance company in the hopes they might choose to pay for the boys' care. As we pursued adoption through all the heartbreaking roadblocks along the way. As we sought guardianship of Geoffrey and Sharon.

We were praying to the God of Ryan to make a way.

* * *

"I wanted to make sure you knew we are serious about you using our guesthouse here in Woodland Hills," my friend Mary Herbert wrote. "It is about fifteen miles to UCLA."

Mary, along with her husband, Mel, and their seventeen-year-old son, Micah, had just returned home to Los Angeles from their first trip to Kenya to visit our family and Living Room.

We met eight years ago after they heard me speak at a church in Los Angeles, and they invited me to their home for lunch. We sat in their backyard surrounded by tall trees and plants of all shades and sizes. They listened to me share about the vision I had to start a hospice home on the other side of the world.

At the end of lunch, Mel looked to Mary and said, "We should be a part of this."

That day, I left with a check in hand to help build Kimbilio Hospice. But much more than that, I had made new friends. Over time, our love and mutual respect had grown deep, and now Mary was inviting my family to come and live in their nearby guesthouse—if the details worked out.

Her email continued, "The guesthouse conversion is small, but I think with some adjustment it could work. When I shared your story with my friend Jaye, the first thing she said was, 'they must come live in the guesthouse.' And as many others were listening to our conversation, friends immediately offered furniture and all matter of things. So, you are very welcome, if that proves to be what you need.

"The outdoor spaces make up for the small interior with plenty of space for everyone. I know this is merely one of the small pieces to this giant puzzle. I wish you could hear how eager people are to walk with you all through this. Your bold steps make everyone bold."

Mary's words were hope as I read them. Her offer was more than a house, as generous as that was in itself. I responded immediately, "If it works for us to come, we would *love* to stay in your guesthouse and be a part of your community."

9

Officially Ours

followed the lead of those around me and bowed as we entered into the judge's chambers. My stomach was churning with nerves and anticipation. While we had been in this office before—multiple times over the past twelve months—today was different. The high court judge sat behind a massive desk ready to hear Ryan's adoption case.

Three hard-fought-for reports sat neatly in a file. By its thickness, it looked as if a small forest had been sacrificed to fill out the necessary paperwork. We crowded into the intimate space. Titus sat beside me, dressed in a suit and tie.

One notable absence from the room was that of our attorney. In the minutes leading up to the scheduled hearing, he was nowhere to be found. His phone was off.

At the last minute, one of the law students interning at his firm arrived with our file and convinced a random attorney in the courthouse—someone we didn't know and who had no familiarity with the case—to represent us.

As ridiculous as that may sound, there was no way we'd ask the hearing to be postponed. We needed to move forward as there were several other battles ahead. To this day, I don't know the stand-in attorney's name or why he was willing to step in on our behalf, but I am grateful all the same.

Four days later, on July 12, 2017, we sat in a courtroom and waited for murder cases to be completed so we could receive our much-awaited ruling. It was Ella's fourth birthday.

"All rise."

I stood and listened as the judge read, "It is hereby ordered and decreed that the applicants be authorized to adopt Ryan Kibichii, a minor born on 3 April, 2016."

All I really heard? Ryan was officially ours.

* * *

The following week, still weary and certainly not yet recovered from the adoption process, Titus and I met with a new attorney. We looked for someone more reliable and knowledgeable regarding guardianship. We had no interest in repeating the last experience.

It only took a few minutes with Ms. Chumba to know she was the right choice. She listened well, asked necessary questions, and seemed to understand what was required for the process. She especially appeared to care about the outcome. The court would soon go on a month-long recess, so Ms. Chumba wanted to present the case immediately.

She asked for a long list of documents, all of which we had just used for the adoption case. She also needed Geoffrey and Sharon's aunt and uncle to give consent for the kids to travel for treatment, which required us becoming legal guardians. "With their consent and these supporting documents," Ms. Chumba said confidently, "I can get the order."

The next morning, we went to Ms. Chumba's office with the children's aunt and uncle for them to give consent. From our previous experience, we expected the court process to last months. The court would send us back to Mr. John's office to get another report.

As much as I didn't want to go back there again, I understood that Ryan's treatment was only possible if Sharon came along. In the same way, Geoffrey's survival was dependent on a few people in powerful positions recognizing his worth and the importance of the treatment.

Later that afternoon, while we were in the grocery store, Titus' phone rang. He answered it and immediately stopped walking. He was nodding his head.

"Who is it?" I prodded.

Titus didn't answer me, just kept nodding and smiling.

"What is happening?" I asked. He simply smiled at me.

When he hung up, Titus calmly explained that it was our attorney who had called. "She submitted the paperwork, and the judge granted the court order for guardianship and permission for Geoffrey and Sharon to travel. She is going to pick up the order from the court now."

"What?!" I said in disbelief. "It's already finished? Titus, are you sure?"

He smiled. "Juli, it's done."

I never dreamed the court order would be signed, sealed, and delivered on the very same day. We didn't have to appear in court. We didn't have to go back to Mr. John and plead for help. No one was questioning our motives, nor were we expected or coerced to pay any bribes.

There were many mountains that felt insurmountable. We often asked God to either move them or give us the wisdom, courage, and strength to climb them.

On this day—in the most surprising way—God had moved one for us.

* * *

"Sharon, do you remember when we all went to the doctor's office, and they swabbed your cheek?" She nodded her head. "The results came back, and your blood matches both Geoffrey's and Ryan's. It isn't a match for Alice. No one's was."

I tried to keep my explanations simple and to the point. There would be time ahead to explain how much this meant, and how much it would cost her.

"Sharon, would you be willing to give a little bit of your blood to help your brothers?"

"Yes," was all she said. She saved her questions for another day.

* * *

Passports were next on my map.

Titus spent days traveling across the country to hand-carry documents from one department to the next. I remained at home trying to get our house in order, packing and repacking in case we got the passports soon and were granted US visas. These would be the final two steps before we could leave.

It was a Tuesday afternoon when Titus let me know that the children's passports were ready. On Wednesday morning, I requested an expedited medical visa appointment. The US embassy responded immediately, granting us an appointment for 7:30 the very next morning. But the US embassy is in Nairobi, and we would normally have to travel by plane to get there.

There were no available flights that evening or the next morning. So, Sharon, Geoffrey, Ryan, Senge, and I jumped in a shuttle van for the eight-hour trip to the capital where we would meet up with Titus.

The night was short and filled with nervous energy, the expectation of what the morning might hold. Would they say yes, trusting the hard-to-believe story we were trying to live out?

We arrived early for our appointment and waited in line with men, women, and children who for varying reasons were requesting to travel to the USA. Several of them were given pink papers, indicating their applications had been denied.

We understood their disappointment well. Ten months ago, when Ryan was six months old, he also received the same slip of pink paper. Back then, we had hoped to take Ryan to a stateside children's hospital for treatment, but the interviewer that day wasn't convinced it was necessary.

We hoped and prayed that today would be different.

As we waited for our turn, Ryan was restless and Geoffrey, as usual, was charming. Our number was called. I exhaled. This was it.

Titus, Senge, Sharon, Geoffrey, Ryan, and I all made our way to the counter where a glass barrier separated us from him. Geoffrey stumbled but quickly picked himself back up again, as he often does.

I held Ryan in my arms as we crowded into a small space, trying to explain concisely, to make sense of why we needed these children to be allowed to travel to America.

David Tarus often jokes that it is easier to go to heaven than it is to get a visa to visit America. For various reasons, this has been the experience of many. But on this day, there was a man who listened to our story.

He looked Sharon in the eyes when she explained that she was going to America to give her blood to help save her brothers. Her English was broken, but her message was clear.

He asked the appropriate questions and, in the end, granted the visas, giving our boys a chance to live.

I am pretty sure the imprint we left on him during those fifteen minutes was minuscule in comparison to what he gave us, but for the man who stood behind that glass window, I will forever be grateful.

* * *

A year of knocking on government doors, navigating unknown systems, asking and advocating, seeking court orders, attending hematology clinics, caring for sick kids, choosing a treatment center, securing visa appointments, and obtaining insurance was finally over.

For almost a year, the goal of receiving medical care for the boys seemed like a long shot, improbable at best. But this was finally our next step.

For all that was still ahead of us, Mary said, "Just come. We'll figure it out."

10

To the Moon

The distance from Eldoret, Kenya, to Los Angeles, California, is 9,490 miles. For many months, the probability of us reaching LA felt as likely as traveling to the moon.

The chasm separated by disparities in prognosis, court documents that were just beyond reach, and embassies and visas that defined who would be allowed to cross the borders.

Meanwhile, in our little orange home in a village in Kenya, two hurting little boys had a sister with blood that perfectly matched theirs. Only, hers was free of sickling cells.

On September 17, 2017, as our family of seven prepared to say good-bye to our home and community to begin—or maybe just continue—an adventure of epic proportions, Los Angeles was no longer a trip to the moon. It was simply a day away.

Seven airplane tickets from Eldoret to Los Angeles were in hand. Functionally, they were one-way tickets as we had no idea when we might return. Would it be six months? Nine? One year later? We didn't know. We were in uncharted territory, entering a storyline where the script was yet to be written.

We carried with us a large green folder overflowing with passports and court orders, medical paperwork, and proof of insurance. It also contained birth certificates and death certificates, US visas, and immunization records. This folder represented countless hours of battling on behalf of these little ones, filled with paperwork to support our far-fetched story.

Our suitcases were packed. Saying good-bye to family and friends, it was time to leave our life's work into trusted hands. We were stepping further into the unknown with the hope of what this journey might hold for the boys, for our family. Perhaps for the world.

Alice would stay behind with her remaining brothers and sisters. The support of our Living Room team was with them, but it was hard to leave her, not knowing if she would still be here when we came back.

On the night before we traveled, a group of our neighbors came over to share a meal at our home. The rain was pouring on our tin roof, and I overheard Sharon talking to her baby brother as she pushed him on Ella's pink tricycle. "God is good, Ryan. He is good all the time."

I don't know what prompted Sharon to say this, but her words settled into my soul.

It wasn't a pat answer to minimize the hard of this world, the hard of our lives. It was spoken by a child who had lost both her parents to death. A child who was preparing to give part of herself to save her sick brothers. A child who somehow had not lost hope or faith amid poverty, injustice, and grief. Instead, she said again, "God is good, Ryan."

We were leaving so much of what we loved in order to say yes to what we hoped was the next right thing to do. Even though I didn't know what was ahead, like Sharon's words, I trusted that the goodness of God would follow us wherever we would go.

* * *

The sun was setting as we walked across the runway and prepared to step into the forty-four-seat propeller plane that would soon be taking off from Eldoret. There was much we were leaving behind and much awaiting us on the other side of the world.

Four little ones were wide-eyed, taking in the newness, the bigness of everything, and thrilled to fly in the *ndege*. They had little comprehension of the long hours, multiple flights, and time changes that were ahead. Ryan was awake within my arms, and I was overwhelmed by the hope that the next time we landed on this runway, he and his brother could be freed from the pain and disease of sickle cell.

On our first forty-five-minute flight to Nairobi, there weren't any seats together and no one was willing to move.

Senge sat with Geoffrey on her lap, even though he was over two years old and had a seat of his own. Sharon sat by herself a few rows in front of me, and I held Ryan on my lap before passing him back to Titus who was a few rows behind me. And Ella, who was barely four, sat all the way in the back of the airplane by herself. She was seated next to a nun who seemed to listen to Ella's tales for the entire plane ride. I kept turning around nervously to check on her, and Ella just smiled and gave me a thumbs up, unfazed.

Upon arriving at Nairobi, our friend Caleb—a Kenya Airways pilot—met us at the airport. He showed up in solidarity to help us carry our bags and to accompany us through the sometimes-complicated process of security. His presence a tangible reminder we were not alone.

A string of flights led us across oceans and continents. As to be expected, it seemed like those flights might never end. At one point, Senge said, "If we were on a bus, I would get off and go home." She probably wasn't joking.

Much greater than any tiredness, I was filled with an overriding sense of marvel at the months of hoping and praying—against all sorts of odds—for this opportunity. And now it was ours.

I walked up and down the aisles of the airplane holding Ryan, trying to get him to fall asleep. I looked around as fellow passengers slept or passed the time by staring at screens. Some were annoyed by their seat assignment or the lack of meal choices.

They didn't know our story, the wonder of the little boy I held within my arms. They didn't know we were in search of miracles, on our way to a land that wasn't our home but was willing to receive us with a love both deep and wide. They didn't know, but as I walked up and down the airplane aisle, I recognized the sacredness of a seemingly normal day and held it in my heart.

After thirty-six hours of travel, we were welcomed to Los Angeles with wide-open arms by our friends Kathy and Mary. Our family divided into two, and we filled car seats to head to our temporary home at Mary and Mel's where we planned to stay for two or three weeks while renovations of the guesthouse were being completed.

We arrived at their yellow home on a cool September afternoon as the sun was preparing to set.

***

We had made it, unsure exactly of what that meant. But somehow, all the miles walked, the hurdles crossed, the tears cried, the doors knocked on, permission denied and granted, this was where the journey had led us. Here. To a home where friends were willing to make space for us.

The guesthouse, a ten-minute walk from the main house, was gutted from top to bottom when we arrived. While the contractor believed he could have it finished and livable within a couple of weeks, Mary was wading through the city permitting process.

Their four-bedroom house was accustomed to their family of three, but they were letting it stretch to hold the hopes and fears of a family in need.

Mel and Mary's room was located on the south side of the home, and Micah's bedroom sat directly beside it.

Another bedroom, next to Micah's, connected by a bathroom in the middle. That was where Sharon, Ella, and Geoffrey would sleep. It had two twin beds with bright sheets and colorful quilts, as well as a third cozy nest constructed on the floor with a mattress in the corner. A vibrant, hand-painted cloth banner hung on the closet door. It read: *Karibu.* Welcome.

On the west side of the house, a sunroom faced the backyard. It had long been Mary's art studio, but she converted it into a bedroom for Senge.

In the middle of the house was a living room with naturally lit spaces from windows and skylights as well as access to a spacious backyard. Artwork filled the walls. There were nooks for sitting or lounging, a bean bag chair on the floor. Beautiful potted plants created green spaces in all directions. Books and toys lined the room.

On the east side of the living room, next to the front door, was a dining room and a kitchen.

And on the north end of the house was the fourth bedroom and bathroom where Titus and I would sleep with a Pack 'n Play set up in the corner for Ryan.

Just outside of our room was a side door, almost always left unlocked to welcome "the high schoolers" in the early morning and again after school.

Mary described this wonderful motley crew of teenage girls and boys, who showed up Monday through Friday to eat a meal, take a nap, or work on homework, simply as the high schoolers. They were friends of Micah's who shared his love for running and were a part of the cross-country team.

Mel and Mary didn't intentionally set out to have an afterschool program for fifteen to twenty youth every day, but in the same way as they now were welcoming us, they kept welcoming them, creating a place that was safe and nurturing, a second home. They didn't make a big deal out of it, just made themselves available and left the door unlocked with food on the counter.

The morning after we arrived, we held a family meeting where the seven of us gathered in the backyard to establish ground rules. For the weeks we would be in the Herberts' home, we wanted to be respectful and honoring of their space and time.

Titus explained to the kids, "We want to leave a light footprint in this home."

It was such a beautiful idea, in theory.

11

Grace

"Mary, Ryan has a fever," I said hesitantly, not wanting it to be true. It was only our second morning in Los Angeles. Our suitcases were still packed, and we were all losing the battle to jet lag. Geoffrey and Ella had just gone back to sleep after playing in the middle of the night, the ten-hour time difference taking its toll.

Mary looked up from her computer screen perched on the kitchen island, a cup of morning coffee in hand. Both Mary and Mel had worked in clinical emergency medicine for decades. They were gurus in the field—Mary as a nurse practitioner and Mel as a physician. Now, they run an extensive online education company that serves emergency medicine doctors around the world.

"Mel," she called. He retreated from his office in the back. "It's time to go to work. Ryan has a fever."

"Oh boy," said Mel in his Australian accent. The three of us knew a trip to the ER was at hand, and admission was almost guaranteed. In a child with sickle cell disease, fever was never taken lightly.

"Where should I take him?" I asked, trying to get my bearings on where we were and what was presently needed.

"I'll take you if you want," Mel volunteered. His calendar was already filled with meetings for the day. He could have quickly assessed Ryan and sent us on our way. Instead, Mel strapped the car seat into the back of his white Tesla and drove us to the community hospital down the road in Tarzana, calling the head of the department before we arrived to alert the team to be ready to receive us.

It soon became clear that if you need to go to an ER, go with Mel. He's kind of a rock star in the emergency medicine world. Once we got past the waiting area, the other doctors came to say hello, to introduce themselves, and explain how much they loved listening to his podcasts.

Meanwhile, I was trying to answer hard questions like, "How many children do you have?" and "Does your house have a smoke alarm?"

The night before we left Kenya, Titus and I stood in our kitchen talking about life and how it looked so different than we imagined it would.

At one point, I paused, as if I had found the words I was searching for, but more likely I finally felt free to say them out loud: "Titus, I am tired from the weight of making medical decisions. I don't know how to do that on top of being their mom."

For months, there was pressure on me to manage my children's illness. To an extent, there was outside help, but I was on the frontline, constantly trying to discern when we needed it. I didn't want to miss anything, but there was a lot going on all around us. From day to day, it was unpredictable as to what would come next. Fevers. Infection. Trouble breathing. Pain. So often pain.

Thirty-six hours into our stay in California, Ryan was admitted to the hospital with a nasty, antibiotic-resistant urinary tract infection. I sat next to Mel and already knew more clearly why we had come to America. For six hours that day, Mel waited patiently with Titus and me.

"I am sorry Ryan's sick," he said. "I know you guys are tired and need a break."

While I hated that he was sick, I also felt relief. There was a team now to help take care of Ryan. And I was grateful—deeply grateful—we had access to it.

* * *

And so, barely a day into our stay in California, I stepped out of the Herbert home for eight days to be in the hospital with Ryan, leaving Senge and Mary, or as we called her, Mama Micah[13]— who barely knew each other's names—to care for the three other children. Only one of the three kids spoke English, and she had enough energy and curiosity to power through the world. And one had sickle cell disease. Meanwhile, Titus went between the home and the hospital, neither of us grasping at that moment how these back-and-forth trips would come to mark our days in Los Angeles.

---

13 According to Kenyan tradition, Mel and Mary would go by Baba and Mama Micah, because their firstborn child is named Micah. Throughout the rest of the book, depending on the circumstances, I use these names interchangeably.

Any sense of control I had come with was finished. Used up. Aspirations of proper meal planning and the vision for leaving a light footprint in the Herbert home was gone. This was real life, and it was anything but simple. Mama Micah was right in describing it as a wild ride.

Sharon was eleven, experiencing life for the first time outside of the village that had raised her. She spoke almost no English but was inquisitive and engaged, taking in a new world much bigger than she had known before—a world of tall buildings, city landscapes, and electricity. A world where there seemed to be enough.

She wondered about the swimming pool in the backyard—it was like a river but different. But so was everything else. Water came from a faucet and was drinkable. There was food—even if she didn't know what all of it was—on the counters and in a refrigerator. There were books to read and papers to draw on. And high schoolers who showed up to sit beside her and color.

Even though she was the oldest of the four kids, she wasn't the firstborn. For now, Sharon was willing to let Ella be in charge—which was good, because Ella wasn't ready to give that up.

Ella was four, but I forgot sometimes how little she still was. She was strong, articulate, and fearless, even when she should have been afraid. We never wondered what she was feeling as she had the words to tell us and did so with vigor and volume.

Mama Micah sent text messages to the hospital throughout the day to report on how Ella and the others were doing, "Ella says she can't sleep on the couch. There's no mosquito net, and she might get malaria."

About Geoffrey, Mama Micah wrote, "I think Geoffrey is eating too many bananas." I read the text and imagined two or three bananas, and I thought maybe we could let it slide.

She texted again, "I think he's eaten seven today."

I laughed out loud and replied, "Yes, that might be too many." I have lived in Kenya for years, but one of the things that always breaks my heart is the ravenous way a child who is familiar with hunger eats, always afraid there won't be more.

Early on with Geoffrey, we needed to tell him to slow down, "There's enough. You can have more in a little bit." It took time for his mind to comprehend, time for his stomach to believe us.

In those early days, Geoffrey often looked at a *World Vision* magazine he found on Mama Micah's coffee table. Instead of showing shock or despair at the poverty within the images, it was as if Geoffrey was looking for a picture of himself. He was looking for his brothers and sisters, studying each page filled with black-skinned children with big smiles as they posed while holding their goats or chickens.

It was familiar for him, like the bananas he consumed in excess.

* * *

I needed a break from the hospital room and decided to go downstairs to get some food. I entered the elevator, and I am not sure what prompted me to read the sign on the door, but its message read, "Should this elevator door fail to open, do not become alarmed. There is little danger of running out of air or the elevator dropping uncontrollably."

Oh my gosh! What? My jaw dropped, and I laughed nervously. In all my life, I had never imagined oxygen being sucked out of an elevator or dropping to my death, but now the idea was planted in my head, even if there was "little danger."

Caring for our children with sickle cell disease felt a bit like this, a constant awareness of what could go wrong, but instead of the danger being little, it was large and looming. And it was very real. Part of my journey was learning to not get swallowed up by fear each time we entered an elevator—even when it was scary.

* * *

Little by little, as the antibiotics cleared the infection from Ryan's body, he became a toddler once more, wanting to play and explore the hospital room. He crawled under the crib to sit in the basket below—as if to hide. Wearing his cartoon-print hospital gown, Ryan would sit on his IV pole as fluids ran into his arm, his small self peering from the room into the enormous hospital corridor.

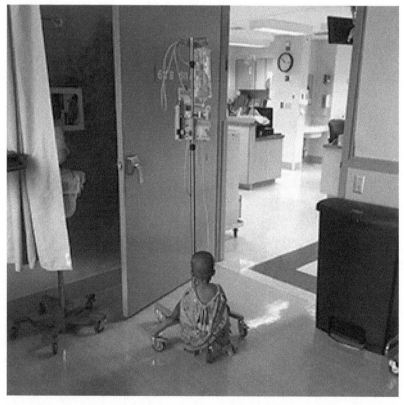

Worlds away from life as Ryan had known it

I had no way of knowing what thoughts filled his mind. I had trouble enough understanding my own, except that the image felt familiar. It was like that future memory of my children being in the hospital in their little gowns. This moment wasn't all three of them, but I watched my baby and prayed that, someday soon, he would be freed from this.

Back when Ryan was seven months old, he started saying a few words at a time and would often parrot us, but at some point along the way, due to all the pain, he pretty much stopped talking altogether. Silence became his language.

I tried to understand what it was he was silently saying. In addition to his lack of words, Ryan had not yet learned to walk by the time we arrived in Los Angeles. Every time he would get close to his first steps, a pain crisis arose, so he refused to put weight on his hurting feet.

When we were back at Mama Micah's, Ryan was ready to take a stab at walking. The high schoolers were his cheerleaders as our seventeen-month-old practiced walking in Mama Micah's kitchen.

This time, he succeeded.

* * *

The day after Ryan was discharged from the hospital, we went for our first appointment with the transplant team at UCLA. Mel offered to drive us again, and we gratefully accepted. We met in the kitchen at 6 a.m. to leave for an 8:00 appointment.

In Los Angeles, drive time does not directly correlate with the distance you need to travel, especially when the 101 and 405 freeways are on your route. They are monsters that can hold you hostage for hours, even if you only need to go a few miles.

The distance from the Herbert house to the hospital in Westwood was fifteen miles. This meant that during off-peak hours, which rarely exist, it took twenty minutes to get to the hospital. In morning and evening traffic times, we were looking at a minimum of an hour's drive. Sometimes two.

Patience was required, so I sang the song I learned as a child to my children—as well as to myself—over and over again:

> *Have patience, have patience*
> *Don't be in such a hurry*
> *When you get impatient, you only start to worry*
> *Remember, remember that God is patient too*
> *And think of all the times when others have to wait for you*

* * *

UCLA Medical Center is a ten-story structure with four towers staggered to create bright, open spaces. It felt big and daunting but also reassuring that it was up to the task of caring for our boys. The third and fifth floors of the hospital were home to the UCLA Mattel Children's Hospital. These would soon become our spaces.

At our first appointment, we met with members of the transplant team for nearly four hours. They were strangers in white coats who came in and out of our white-walled exam room, one by one, to thoroughly review the boys' medical history and to listen to our story.

These doctors explained in detail the expected road leading up to hospitalization—the screening process for Ryan, Geoffrey, and Sharon. There was much discussion again about all the risks of treatment.

The phrase *life-threatening* was used more than a few times, but in the end, Dr. Moore, the head of the transplant team, said soberly, "It is my strongest recommendation you move forward with this treatment."

With all its risks, the life-threatening treatment was still the best opportunity for our kids to have health and life. We believed this coming into the appointment, and we left with more information about the hard realities that awaited us and greater hope for the cure we were seeking.

The team required that we do one transplant at a time, beginning with Ryan. Because he was the youngest, the doctors believed he had less risk of complications. If all went well, Geoffrey would begin his transplant one hundred days later.

I sat with all the information and wondered—*How do you prepare your heart and mind to give your children chemotherapy? To plan for the hard and the unknown, to barely comprehend that you are about to go to the very edge of life, taking all the risk upfront, with the expectation and hope it will bring freedom and healing. What would the road to get there involve? What if the story doesn't go as you had hoped? What if you are trading their hurts for more suffering? What if death comes?*

There was limited space within my heart to wrestle through these questions. Titus and I wanted everything to be alright as quickly as possible. But there was very little we could control or fix.

Oh, I grieved frivolous things like Ryan's beautiful eyelashes that would soon fall out. I fixated on warm, coat-style pajamas and beanies, wanting him to be warm enough. I planned for the nest I hoped to create, but would it be enough to keep Ryan safe?

Meanwhile, I packed and prepared to be separated from Ella, as she, and eventually Sharon, would go to spend months with my parents while Ryan was in the hospital. It was a lot for this mama's heart.

In the days leading up to the transplant, a long checklist of screening tests for Ryan, Geoffrey, and Sharon was completed, and, one by one, specialists were consulted. The dentist found several cavities in Geoffrey's baby teeth, one involving his two front teeth. They needed to be treated before proceeding with his transplant.

The dentist said, "This should be easy-peasy, Geoffrey!" She looked at me and continued, "I recommend we use silver fluoride. It will kill the bacteria and harden the remaining tooth, with the goal being to stop the active cavity. The only thing is, it will turn his teeth black."

In the bigger scheme of things, having Geoffrey's front teeth turn black was a simple decision, an easy-peasy, "Oh, okay."

Eventually, after many appointments with doctors and what seemed like every lab test known to man had been run, a request was submitted and approved by our insurance to go ahead with the transplants.

A start date was put on the calendar for Ryan, only to be pushed back after he developed a cold. The season remained predictably unpredictable. Most things needed to be held lightly. Within all our plans, we had to leave room for interruption.

* * *

The "easy guesthouse renovation" was also on a schedule of its own. There were delays in the approvals from the city, and then we received shocking news of the sudden death of the architect. This caused the process of seeking permits to essentially start over. While our family remained in their home, Mama Micah worked endlessly to move the project forward, but it would not budge.

Our two-week stay in their house had turned into a month and was approaching two, with no end in sight.

The Herberts were wonderful to live with, generous with their space and time. But our kids were loud and uncontainable. Between their extensive medical needs that involved pretty much daily owies for Geoffrey and repeat hospitalizations for Ryan, and a spirited Ella who every so often would turn into "Rosie the Jaguar," we failed at our small footprint intention.

* * *

Ella pursued knowing everyone's name. She was the first to stand at the back door when it was time to leave for school each morning. She would put her backpack on and lead the Kenyan kids in shouting every high schooler's name as they threw on their backpacks and scampered to class.

She engaged with the high schoolers after school, admiring the shirts they wore or their earrings. She watched them all.

I remember the day she said, "He matches me," pointing to the skin of one of the high schoolers. They put their arms side by side, and she smiled. She had gotten it right. They matched.

There is a part of our Western thinking that often dismisses adolescents as too much to deal with, but there was a magic that the high schoolers carried. They were fluent in the language of kid.

All those months earlier, when Dr. Jodi said, "You will need community to survive," I never imagined it would look like this.

* * *

Our dear Ella thrives with firm boundaries, something that was nearly impossible to provide in a season that didn't lend itself to routine. With all the changes, Ella often articulated her concerns, and everyone in the house was fully aware of them.

It ached this mama's heart to leave her to go to the hospital and have her ask questions like, "Mommy, where are you going? Again? Can you tell the doctor you need to come home to see your Ella? When can it be my turn?"

Ella was homesick for Africa. When we went outside one night, Ella asked, "Mama, can we look at the stars? Wait, Mama, where are the stars? We have stars in Kenya. Is that a star? Oh no, Mama, that is an airplane."

Other times, she sang at the top of her lungs, "I want to go home, to my home in Kenya. I want to go hooooooome!" And then she whispered—which was unusual for Ella—"Mama, Ryan misses his home in Kenya. You know how he cries a lot. It's because he misses his friends." She continued, "And when he hits other children, it's not appropriate, but he's still a good boy. He just wants to go home."

She missed her friends. The beauty. The simplicity. The guava trees that fill our yard. The sounds of birds singing throughout the day and ten thousand crickets chirping at night. She missed walking to school and passing by the cows she knew by name.

In truth, the rest of us—the less-vocal ones—missed our home in Kenya. While we were unbelievably grateful for the opportunity for our boys to receive treatment, Ella said what we all felt but could not say. We missed Kenya.

* * *

One Sunday evening dinner found our family all home together. A peace filled me when four little plates sat in a row. Something felt complete. Ryan had been discharged from the hospital again only the day before, and we were already anticipating the next admission. This time, it would be for his transplant.

Ella would soon go to stay with my parents in Redding, a city in Northern California. Sharon would follow weeks later—after the bone marrow harvest was complete. But tonight, a new friend, Ms. Jaye, graciously brought over a delicious meal for all to enjoy. Her kindness was another reminder of the gift of community.

As we shared supper, Mel's cousin Ceci came to visit us with her warm sense of loving-kindness. She sat on the floor with our children and sang about the sweetness of grace. The sound of her voice was as beautiful as the message.

Sharon was strumming the guitar with Ceci while Ryan clapped along from his highchair in delight. Senge fed him a bite of rice and stew, and then another. Ryan seemed to take in everything good about the moment.

Ella was asleep in her bed by 7 p.m., exhausted from her day's adventures, her "science experiences"—mixing Mama Micah's colorful flowers and green leaves into magic potions—and her unrelenting chase of Lightning and Giza, two of the Herberts' household pets.

Geoffrey filled my lap. Micah once said, "When you've been hugged by Geoffrey, you've really been hugged." He leans in and holds on tight for a long time. It was some sort of therapy for him and for whoever was lucky enough to have him in their arms.

This night, as the room resonated with the gift of singing, Geoffrey's left foot was paining once again, as sickled cells cruelly clumped in his foot.

"Ouchie!" He used his newly acquired word almost daily, unfortunately. "Bandages" was another. He needed them—lots of them—to try and cover up the pain. The singing went on:

> Through many dangers, toils, and snares,
> I have already come;
> 'Tis grace hath brought me safe thus far,
> And grace will lead me home.

Grace had indeed brought us. And grace would lead us.
Deep breath in.

I asked Geoffrey if he wanted to be wrapped onto my back and carried. This posture soothed him and his baby brother, as it does many children all over the world. This mama's back was a safe, comforting place for Geoffrey. We walked and walked until the pain eased and Geoffrey found respite in sleep.

> The Lord has promised good to me.
> His word my hope secures.
> He will my shield and portion be,
> As long as life endures.[14]

In all the watching and waiting, we took in the grace that permeated the steps of our story while asking for freedom from the owies.

The disease had to die for this to be possible.

---

14 "Amazing Grace" by John Newton, 1772.

12

Let the Healing Begin

A sliver of a moon remained in the dark sky on the Monday morning of Thanksgiving week as we walked deeper into the unknown. It was time for Ryan to begin his transplant journey. I whispered words my soul longed to be true: *Let the healing begin.*

I was not asking for ease or comfort, while I wholeheartedly welcomed it. Mostly, I wanted new life. And I wanted protection over little hearts and minds that could not grasp what was happening, and for bigger ones like mine that weren't that much further ahead.

Ryan had a 5 a.m. call time for surgery to place a central line within his chest. He was surprisingly happy to be awake, even though it was early, and he was hungry. But our little boy was preoccupied with a red wagon that filled the hallway in the preoperative unit. He climbed in and out, proud of his discovery.

My attention turned to another baby, maybe a year old, in the waiting bay across from ours. He had big, beautiful brown eyes, much like Ryan's, and was also preparing to go into surgery.

It was the look on his mama's face that moved me—a mixture of love and angst—as her child was taken from her arms and rolled down the hallway. Her pain felt deeply familiar, a reminder of my own. A few minutes passed and then it was my turn to do the same painful routine—let go of Ryan and walk away.

While we waited for him to return from surgery, Titus and I moved into our temporary home: Room 3525. As we walked onto the transplant floor, a teenage girl was being wheeled down the hallway. Her eyes were tired, her body still weak. But she was heading home. We sensed the relief and elation of her family as they carried bags of accumulated belongings toward the elevator. I didn't know their story, but something about their joy nearly undid me.

I silently celebrated whatever victory it was they held today, hoping one day it would be ours too.

Dr. Federman and the transplant team came into the room and explained once again that Ryan would begin the conditioning regimen tonight. "Conditioning," we came to learn, was a kind and sterile term for nine days of grueling chemotherapy leading up to transplant. Dr. Federman described this time as a process of "making space."

"Ryan's bone marrow needs to be wiped out to create room for his sister's to come in," he said. A combination of loss, love, and sacrifice was required for this treatment to be possible.

Dr. Federman apologized that we would be in the hospital for Thanksgiving, but I assured him this was why we had come all the way, crossing oceans and barriers of all kinds. We wanted a chance for Ryan to be free of this disease.

* * *

An hour later, Ryan was wheeled into the room on a gurney, drowsy from the anesthesia, with a teddy bear wearing blue scrubs tucked by his side. He was hungry, and as I prepared to give him milk, the resident doctor returned, explaining there was some sort of mistake in the OR. The wrong central line had been placed in Ryan's chest. "Don't feed him," he said. "He may need to go back to surgery."

"What?" I asked. "He has to go back to surgery? We can't use the line that was already placed?"

I blurted out all three questions before giving him a chance to respond. This was the same resident who, while introducing himself a few minutes ago, told me about a hierarchy on the pediatric floor, something about nurses being toward the bottom, clearly below him. As a nurse practitioner, I realized he still had a few more things to learn about how hospitals run and the role of nurses within patient care.

About the time I finished my line of questions, the surgeon walked into our room, a quiet and serious man, still dressed in his surgical scrubs. He looked me in the eyes with a sense of humility and sincerity and apologized for the error.

"While in the OR," he began, "I don't know how it happened, but I picked up a dialysis catheter instead of the type your son needs. I am sorry for my mistake. I've discussed with the transplant team, and we've decided to leave the line in as it will still work for his treatment needs."

"Thank you for your honesty," I said. "We all make mistakes sometimes."

His transparency felt as surprising to me as the error itself. There are countless checks and rechecks that take place within an OR—the error should not have happened. But he could have brushed it off as not a big deal or blamed someone else for how or why it occurred. Instead, he took responsibility.

The integrity of the moment, if anything, increased my trust in the team and the care that would be provided to our sons.

* * *

I started a paper chain out of a rainbow of colored construction paper that evening and wrote the words that were echoing within me all day, "Day minus-10: Let the healing begin." The idea was to add a slip of paper each day to mark the time Ryan spent in the hospital. We didn't know how many days it would be, but I wanted a visual reminder of this season.

The idea was the reverse tradition of something my family did each Christmas when I was a child. We built a chain of alternating red and green links on December 1, and we took one slip of paper off the chain until there was no more, and Christmas came.

On this night, there was a single link as chemotherapy began to flow through Ryan's dialysis line. He slept unaware as I lay on a couch beside him, listening to the IV pump infuse powerful chemicals throughout his body.

I drifted in and out of sleep as the lights from Westwood shone outside through the window on the streets below. Ryan's nurse quietly came in and out to check on our boy. There was no turning back at this point.

Day minus-9. I walked into a large children's playroom filled with the aroma of home and Thanksgiving. Tired moms and dads with children in the hospital—just like ours—gathered for an early Thanksgiving dinner of turkey, mashed potatoes, and the works.

I quietly held my plate in front of me as I walked along a serving line. A teenage boy in a green-and-blue plaid flannel shirt placed green beans on my plate, and tears filled my eyes. The tears surprised both of us, overflowing one large drop at a time. I felt exposed without any way to hide.

My tears didn't stem from a place of sadness or grief—while that would have been appropriate. Instead, they were linked to the kindness of the boy with the green beans—I knew it through and through. I'd spent so much of my life wanting to have it all together, to be the one serving, giving, noticing.

As a nurse, I'd always been a helper, but it was my turn to learn to receive. The vulnerability of suffering was lending me a taste for kindness, for supposedly mundane, everyday sort of things. My crying was a response, but it also was a form of prayer I didn't learn about in Sunday School. It expressed longing my heart and mind could not find language for.

Thankfully, in those days, I discovered "Kindness," a poem by Naomi Shihab Nye:[15]

> You must wake up with sorrow.
> You must speak to it till your voice
> catches the thread of all sorrows
> and you see the size of the cloth.
> Then it is only kindness that makes sense anymore,
> only kindness that ties your shoes
> and sends you out into the day to mail letters and purchase bread,

---

15   Naomi Shihab Nye, *Words Under the Words: Selected Poems* (Portland: The Eight Mountain Press, 1995).

only kindness that raises its head
from the crowd of the world to say
it is I you have been looking for,
and then goes with you everywhere
like a shadow or a friend.

* * *

A whiteboard in Ryan's room detailed the plans for each day of the conditioning period. A nurse would come for twelve hours at a time to perform superhero tasks in ways that made the hard a little less so. At the beginning of each shift, they updated the care plan on the board.

A list of chemotherapy agents for day minus-10 until day minus-2 were written in colorful markers with boxes to be checked after the day's drugs had been administered. Day minus-1 had REST written beside it, a welcome break before Sharon's marrow would be harvested and transplanted into Ryan. That would be day 0.

The passing days felt a little like living in a time warp as nights and days blended into one another. Uneventful days were the highlights; it felt like grace to have "nothing to write home about." As the boxes on the whiteboard were checked off, I'd add another link of construction paper to my chain and exhale.

Titus and I took turns staying at the hospital, often overlapping during the chemo period. Senge and Mama Micah remained at home caring for Geoffrey and Sharon.

* * *

Ryan tolerated the first days of chemotherapy with little discomfort, but as the toxicity built up in his body, the nausea kicked in, beginning with a confused look in his watering eyes followed by retching and vomiting. I pressed the call light button and a warm, elderly voice from the reception desk filled our room.

"Mrs. Kibichii, this is Mary, how may I help you?" There was no need to correct her about my name. Ryan's last name had not yet been changed to Boit. To explain all of this required more than I had within me.

Except for Mary, everyone else on the floor referred to me as *mom* and Titus as *dad*. I imagine it was the easiest way to communicate with families. Simply identify people by their roles. For me, it felt affirming, after such a long journey, to be known and referred to simply as Ryan's mom.

"Mary, Ryan's vomiting," I said, "Please call his nurse."

"Alright dear, the nurse will be right in," and the speaker clicked off.

The nurse swooped in and added a dose of ondansetron into Ryan's line, humming pleasantly while she did.

Thankfully, it worked, the nausea temporarily suppressed. I welcomed relief from the suffering we were inflicting upon him.

Day minus-6. Ryan's body grew hot with fever as a drug derived from rabbits—for real—flowed through his veins. As I lay quietly beside Ryan's shivering body, I remembered Titus' words about Agui's rabbit story and the need to protect it. Ryan's hospital bed had a green canopy that zipped closed on all sides to protect him from falling. I wanted it to be able to shield him from much, much more.

As the hours ticked on, the medication dripped through the IV until it was finished. Night was approaching, and the day nurse was signing off in the hallway to the nurse coming on for the next twelve hours.

Ryan's eyes rolled back as his body began to seize. I froze momentarily before running into the hallway. "Ryan's having a seizure!"

The night nurse calmly moved with appropriate urgency to assess Ryan while the emergency pediatric team was alerted to come. The seizure that thrashed his helpless body began to resolve. He immediately fell asleep.

Neither Titus nor I wanted to leave Ryan that night; we both remained at the hospital. In the middle of the night, Ryan was rushed for a CT scan of his brain to try and understand the cause of the seizure. Titus accompanied him through the process, and when they returned, he sat in a chair next to Ryan's bed all night long, like a guard on duty, his job to protect his son.

I lay on the couch next to the window exhausted but with eyes wide open. I was afraid, hoping the morning would come with some sort of relief.

Titus and I messaged back and forth with Mary and Mel, explaining the developments. They were experts on everything medical but also safe with the raw, unfiltered parts, of which there were many.

Ryan's hair and beautiful eyelashes fell out in clumps, leaving a trail of tiny black coils within his bed and wherever he went. The cells in his mucosal membranes began to slough off, causing sores that traversed from his lips and mouth all the way to his anus. It was painfully debilitating.

Ryan stopped eating and drinking completely, and he received all nutrients through his central line.

Like clockwork, every night at 2 a.m., the nurse quietly came into Ryan's room and drew his daily labs. His counts, as to be expected, were dropping from the chemo. Depending on the numbers, blood or platelets—or both—were hung to replace what was being depleted.

Ryan's white blood cell count was heading toward zero. As intended, every fighting cell in his body was being erased. They were almost gone, leaving Ryan vulnerable to pathogens from inside and out. Without a controlled environment, it would be impossible for him to survive.

* * *

The transplant floor was a locked unit. At the entrance were double doors with an intercom button and cameras that helped to screen all visitors. Each time I stood at the double doors, waiting for the buzzer indicating the door was unlocked, I'd sanitize my hands. The automated sound of the dispenser accompanied the buzzing of the door.

Inside the unit, animal print wallpaper covered the hallways at children's eye level, and another hand sanitizer dispenser lived at each and every door, as well as on the outside and the inside of all patient rooms.

The doors remained closed, protecting the little ones within their bubble spaces. Sometimes my path crossed with another mama whose eyes were scared or tired. Very often, there were no words to exchange. Other times, I walked past a conversation between a doctor or team of them and parents, their frustration palpable.

Mostly, there was no one to blame for the hurting of their child, but the anger overshadowed the underlying sadness we all felt. They wanted to wake up from the nightmare that seemed to keep on going.

For the most part, we were all on our own journeys, side by side, sharing a hallway at times. But then we went into the room with our child's name written on it and shut the door behind us. We'd use hand sanitizer over and over again, as many times as possible, to do what we could to protect them.

Oh, we heard the sound of crying through the walls. We listened at night to the sounds when the nausea or pain got to be too much. Sometimes those sounds would come from our room. All we could do was listen, pray, and push the call light button, hoping for a reprieve.

* * *

Each morning, a team of doctors stopped by the room to review every child on the unit. Typically, they began at the east end of the hallway and worked their way, one by one, until every child had been assessed.

A group of white coats gathered with computers to look at the latest lab values and tests. It was a teaching hospital with residents still learning their practice. They cycled through the unit on a weekly basis before moving on to another area of specialty. Some were skilled with their medical knowledge but not yet comfortable in their own skin. Others were more ready, humble, and able to look a mama in the eyes, even when it was hard.

The residents were responsible each morning to round on their assigned patients before the larger group met. They presented their findings methodically from head to toe or in systems and made recommendations based on the report. This is how they learned and grew to become skilled clinicians.

Fellows are doctors who have completed years of residency training. Ours were specializing in the care of children with cancer or other blood disorders. These doctors were instrumental in the treatment plan, much more consistent and familiar with the specific needs of transplant kids.

Years of training and practice informed their assessments and decision-making. The fellows were still under the supervision of the attending physician but functioned more reliably and independently.

The attending doctors were in charge. They typically covered the unit for a week before rotating off, when another doctor came on. They listened as the students presented cases, but ultimately, they called the shots on implementing the most appropriate treatment plans for each child.

A pharmacist and nurse typically joined the rounds each morning too. The team welcomed me, as Ryan's mama, to listen in while they discussed his care.

After conversing, the team donned yellow gowns, masks, and gloves to look at the child they had been discussing. To listen and assess, to make sure the clinical picture they were making plans around looked the same as the child within the bed.

What I found remarkable was the number of times, in their busyness, they paused to allow Ryan to be a little boy who had traveled from around the world to receive their care. They noticed pictures on the wall, commented on Ryan's pajamas. He was more than a disease with a prognosis or a bed number; they let him be a child with a name and story.

And I was allowed to be his mom with my own set of hopes and fears.

* * *

Day minus-1. All the chemo boxes had been checked off on the whiteboard. Today was about rest and getting ready for tomorrow's harvest and transplant. I went home to Mama Micah's house for the afternoon while Titus remained with Ryan. I made a last-minute trip to Target for red and pink snowflake pajamas and a sparkly black beanie for Sharon. How could I make her feel cozy, safe, and loved? Another attempt at nesting, even if it was only for an overnight trip.

While Ryan didn't have the words to tell us where it hurt, what he wanted or what he needed, Sharon did. I wanted her to feel safe enough to be able to share—in whatever language or means available to her.

Sharon was ready to give her bone marrow to help save Ryan and Geoffrey, even if she didn't fully understand what was being asked of her. Oh, it had been explained and she had given assent, but it was hard to imagine what she really understood. She was willing to do it, even though it was scary and would hurt.

She brought with her a small duffle bag filled with a soft blanket and slippers and the snowflake pajamas. Her art teachers from a studio nearby lovingly painted a sign with intricate button and beadwork that read: "We heart Sharon." The banner would hang on the wall in Sharon's hospital room, the room next door to her baby brother's.

Because Sharon has sickle cell trait—meaning she is a carrier of the disease without having any symptoms—the goal for Ryan was to give up the disease and exchange it with the trait.

For Sharon, the transplant team boasted of never having had a complication from a donor, and they were committed to keeping this track record. Sharon was admitted to the hospital overnight to receive IV fluids. Tomorrow morning, she would go to surgery to harvest her bone marrow.[16]

---

16 Bone marrow donation is a surgical procedure where doctors use needles to withdraw liquid marrow from both sides of the back of the donor's pelvic bone.

* * *

A lot of juggling was going on these days. Ella stayed with my parents, thriving but also wondering why she wasn't with us.

Geoffrey remained at Mama Micah's, learning to speak English and adapting to a new place where life was a little crazy, but he was loved completely. Mama Micah spent endless hours sitting and playing with Geoffrey, reading him books, and completing art projects.

Senge did a lot of the day-to-day tasks: feeding, bathing, giving Geoffrey medications, placing Band-Aids on the owies, and putting him to bed. She helped keep all our heads above water, quietly filling in countless gaps.

Mama H., a mother of high schoolers, heard about our family from her twin sons, Hayden and Harrison, who often came by Mama Micah's house before and after school. Mama H., a middle school teacher, had lived in Kenya for a couple of years while she was in the Peace Corps. While we didn't ever post a volunteer sign-up form anywhere, Mama H. somehow joined the team and watched for ways to help.

At times, she asked what was needed, but mostly she just made a meal and sent it with the boys. Or sometimes, she delivered the food herself, and when she was over, she sat and played or read a book with Geoffrey. She arranged trips to the Los Angeles Zoo and to Train Town for Geoffrey and Senge.

Within our evolving community, there was a team of people willing to help with the many moving parts. To send a gift card. To deliver a meal at the hospital or home. To remind us in tangible ways that we were not alone.

High schoolers showed up each morning and afternoon, playing with Geoffrey and Sharon, reading a book, doing any task assigned by Mama Micah. And Baba Micah remained on standby, ready to be UberMD as duty called.

Everybody played their part, little by little, to get a monumental job done. It wasn't any of their responsibilities, but every step along the way, love invited them—as it had us—to participate. And we all kept stepping up and saying yes.

The night Sharon was admitted, Baba Micah drove her, Senge, and me to UCLA while Mama Micah stayed with Geoffrey. As we crawled down the freeway, Mel showed Sharon some of the cool tricks of the Tesla. The seat warmers, the drawing options on the screen, the variety of music selections. Distraction at its best, and we all welcomed it.

Upon being admitted to the hospital, Sharon asked to go and visit Ryan. Once given permission, she walked into his room and climbed into Ryan's fort of a bed where she laid down beside him—the look on both of their faces when they saw one another was nothing short of love.

"*Nimekukosa*, Ryan." I've missed you.

I wondered about all that tomorrow would hold. For Sharon. For Ryan. And for Geoffrey, who would get his turn in one hundred days.

13

A New Beginning

D ay 0. A team of doctors came to round in the morning like they always do. Only this time, I had two children for them to review. It was transplant day, a day we had hoped and prayed for with great anticipation.

Mel drove Titus down to be part of the many activities of this landmark day. Mama Micah lovingly remained with Geoffrey, quietly orchestrating all the moving parts, helping to ensure none of the important balls dropped along the way.

When it was time for Sharon to go to the OR, I handed Ryan over to Senge—shortly after he had vomited down my back. I climbed in bed with Sharon, and we waited together in the cold hallway of the second floor, surrounded by Dr. Moore and other doctors.

They marveled at the story that was unfolding—two brothers from Kenya who needed a transplant and a sister who was a willing match. Sharon played Candy Crush on the hospital's iPad, another welcome distraction, as the doctors and I conversed about how we got here.

Before they wheeled Sharon away, I signed one last consent form on behalf of a child who I didn't give birth to but whom I had grown to love.

In the last month, I had done this exercise three times, this "letting go" of Ryan. Now, it was my turn with Sharon. Once again, I felt the deep emotion, the responsibility of having another child go into an OR.

I hugged her as tears filled our eyes. "I will be waiting for you," I said. Her bed was wheeled away, and I was left alone to walk through the white maze of hallways. I found my way back to the elevator that took me to Ryan.

* * *

A decorative sign adorned a bucket outside of his room. It read: Happy birthday, Ryan. In a few hours—because of his sister's sacrifice—in many ways, Ryan would be reborn. I told his nurse Marielle, "I hope today goes better than his original birthday."

On April 3, 2016, Ryan had taken his first breath as his mama prepared to take her last. By a miracle of God, this premature baby survived his first days in the world. On this his second birthday—as they called it—I prayed for new life.

I sat and waited with my friend Kathy while Ryan was asleep in his bed beside us. We talked of the wonder of all that was occurring. It was like how Walter Brueggemann describes, "I am celebrating the impossible that is right before my eyes, even though I can't explain any of it."[17]

Without a trace of regret, I wondered how we got here. *How did these beautiful little people become mine? How did their pain, joy, and healing become part of my story? How did this happen, really?*

I don't pretend to know how heaven works, but I liked the idea of it including a mama and baba watching their little ones with the same sense of love and awe with which I found myself filled on that day at UCLA.

When the harvest was complete, Dr. Moore came into the room with a team of doctors, all still in scrubs from the OR. One of the fellows held a white cooler in her hands. It was filled with bone marrow that would soon flow into Ryan and, one day, into Geoffrey.

I walked back through the white walls of the second floor to find Sharon in a post-operative unit. A teddy bear clothed in pink scrubs sat beside her. Within an hour, Sharon was awake and being transported back to her room.

Senge and our dear friend Koko Debi sat with her while she enjoyed as much ice cream as she wanted. All the while, next door, the transplant team was preparing to transfuse Ryan's little body with his sister's marrow. The doctors and nurses warned us that the transplant often feels anticlimactic for families. I tried to assure them the mantra we were living right now was, *boring is good.*

As the marrow began to flow in the tubing and into Ryan's body, a special clock on the wall was running, documenting for the team how long the transplant process was taking. As a nurse,

---

17   Walter Brueggemann, *Celebrating Abundance: Devotions for Advent* (Louisville: John Knox Press, 2017).

the only time I had noticed these clocks was when something was going terribly wrong, most often during a code.

On this day, though, the clock was welcome. As marrow ran into Ryan's body, Titus played "Taunet Nelel," a song by Kalenjin artist Emmy Kosgei.[18] The translated lyrics say, "It's a new beginning. There's new thinking—look at it! God is saying, 'I am doing a new thing. Don't look back.'"

One hour and fifteen minutes after the transplant began, it was finished. The clock stopped, and now came the waiting and watching, hoping Sharon's marrow would find its home in her brother. We prayed that Ryan would be spared from infection and that the ongoing side effects of the chemotherapy would be minimal.

Sharon waddled her way into her brother's room that evening to sit and hold Ryan, her face puffy and her body sore and tired. Ryan was delighted by her presence, unaware of the gift she had given.

The cells now needed time to find their home in Ryan's body. They were like migrants in a foreign land, the place being a bit hostile and unwelcoming. A medication called tacrolimus—an immunosuppressant—was started to help Ryan's body receive and integrate the cells.

At the very least, it would be ten days before we would begin to see Ryan's white count move from zero. For now, we would wait.

The following day, Sharon returned to Mama Micah's home, sore and swollen. Several high school boys sat beside her on the couch. They were sweaty, having just finished running practice,

---

18 Emmy Kosgei, 2009. *Taunet Nelel*. Emmy Kay.

but they ate mint chocolate chip ice cream together and watched *Barbie*. Her choice. It was an act of solidarity, and she knew it.

* * *

I used to drink tea with milk and a spoonful of sugar. It's the way my mom made it for me growing up, but somewhere amid days and nights of hospital life, I stopped adding sugar to my tea. I don't remember deciding to stop. It wasn't a health-conscience decision. Opening the white paper packets labeled *sugar* and pouring it into a paper cup was an extra step I simply could no longer do.

I was tired of the artificial lights and sounds, the recirculated airflow. My mind couldn't process TV shows or my once-favorite movies. Music—which is usually therapeutic for me—felt hollow. With few exceptions, I preferred silence.

If I was going to take in a book, I couldn't read on a Kindle or my phone. I needed words printed on paper that my hands could touch. I needed to go outside and feel the grass between my toes. To let water wash over my tiredness. My senses longed for authentic stimulation, for beauty, nature, and the sound of laughter to remind me we were all still alive.

And somewhere along the way, I gave myself permission to wear yoga pants for the next year.

* * *

Ryan was supported with platelets and blood products, antibiotics, feedings through his central line, and pain medicine. Everything that went into Ryan needed to come out equally. He was too little to have even small amounts of weight gain from all the supportive care required to keep him alive. Diapers were weighed meticulously, and Ryan was measured both morning and night.

The nurses came in and out of our room, frequently assessing for any changes in Ryan and making recommendations to the doctors and adjustments as needed. They were skilled scientists in a highly specialized field, at times overlooked or underestimated, but they ran the floor. They were the eyes and ears, the hands that made the hospital run on a macro level and who helped my baby live within his little bubble.

We learned their names and bits of their stories as they did the same for us. They were professionals who chose to welcome us into their world, straddling the invisible line between getting a job done, which was essential, and loving their patients, which was kind and brave.

Without warning, the waiting morphed from trying to get through the days to a much scarier path.

On day plus-8, Ryan spiked a fever. Antibiotics were changed to broaden the coverage for infection as Ryan's body didn't have any immunity to fight off even simple, everyday exposures. Blood cultures and nasal swabs were sent to see what might be going on. Also, his daily labs were showing concerning trends. His liver enzymes were starting to rise.

On this night and the next morning, I was scheduled to give a talk at Christian Assembly—my church in Los Angeles since college days—about what it means to live with hope in the middle of the story. Before the healing happens. While there are still unanswered questions. When life feels hard, and you don't know what the outcomes will be.

When I stood up to share on Saturday night, I didn't know that I would *not* be back to speak for Sunday services. I didn't know a greater level of uncertainty and untellable suffering was on its way.

14

Advent Waiting

was at home, awake at 3 a.m. reviewing Ryan's lab results online and saw that his liver enzymes and other labs were increasingly getting worse. I called the hospital, and Ryan's nurse shared that it looked like Ryan was developing a horrific transplant complication known as venous occlusive disease (VOD).

"Ryan's condition is getting worse. I think you and Titus should come," he said. "It looks like his liver is failing, and he's septic with infection." Ryan's nineteen-month old body was having a hard time keeping up with it all.

In the dark of the night, I laid next to Titus trying to wrap my head around all that was going wrong. Ryan's Pack 'n Play sat empty in the corner of our room, waiting for him to come home healed from his disease. He was supposed to get better—that was the only acceptable narrative.

I texted Mama Micah, "Ryan's not doing well. Can we meet in the kitchen?" I sent a similar message to my parents who were in town to see us, asking them to come and help with the kids. A third message went to my pastor to cancel my speaking commitments for the day.

The electric kettle boiled water for an early morning cup of tea. Mary, Mel, and I gathered in the corner of the kitchen. The look on their faces mirrored mine. I tried to explain to Mel what the nurse had said but lacked words. "Mel, his liver is failing. It is something called VOD." This was one of the possible complications we had been told about before; it was unique to transplants.

Ella, Geoffrey, and Sharon played around us, not yet aware of all that was going on in the room. My parents showed up not long after and stood silently beside us. They wanted to help, to understand more of the situation.

I didn't have words to explain. Everything hurt. And I was afraid.

Mel drove Titus and me to the hospital in silence. It was an early Sunday morning, and the traffic on the freeways reflected it. As we made our way onto the transplant unit, the medical team stood outside Ryan's door, the same look in their eyes as we had.

The doctor explained, "There's a lot going on in Ryan right now. His liver is failing. He needs to start a newly approved drug called defibrotide, but there is a high risk of bleeding with the medication. Because Ryan also seems to have an infection, most likely from a virus, this is a very complicated situation. We are going to monitor him closely today. It's likely he'll need to be transferred to the PICU."[19]

I nodded, taking in the gravity of his words. When we opened the door to Ryan's room, he was laying in his little green fort. I heard the sound of his labored breathing from the other side of the room and rushed to his side.

His cheeks were red and chafed, rubbed raw from the drooling related to mucositis, his belly taut from the fluids accumulating in his abdomen. His hands and feet were ice-cold as I placed them in my hands.

I fixated on this, even though there were a hundred other things to notice. Ryan's cold extremities felt like death to me. It's something I often saw in my hospice patients. Ryan's blood circulation was now focused on preserving his internal organs.

My gaze pivoted between a monitor displaying Ryan's heart rate, blood pressure and oxygen saturation, and his sick body in front of me. IV tubes of antibiotics and blood products were infusing into his chest. Ryan cried, his voice hoarse, and Titus immediately scooped him up into his arms, careful not to pull on the wires and tubing connected to Ryan's body.

Ryan leaned his face against Titus' chest. His eyes were open, but the light within them seemed all but gone. A blanket my sister had quilted for Ryan with orange, gold, and green fabric squares rested across Titus' lap as he sat, silent and resolute, completely available to the needs of his son.

I hugged Senge in the corner of the room, thanking her for being with Ryan. She quietly packed her few belongings. Last night had been too much to ask of her. Mama Micah waited downstairs

---

19 The pediatric intensive care unit (PICU) specializes in caring for critically ill children.

to drive her home. I dropped onto the couch next to the window, trying to make sense of what was happening.

Mel sat in another corner, eyes glued to his phone, reading everything published about VOD. I chose not to look. I didn't want to see the statistics or know the odds of whether my child might live or die, especially when I already understood they were not good.

I needed Mel to help us hold it together, to guide us with the appropriate questions to ask the doctors, to tell me only what was needed for the moment.

I was not in denial. My mind and heart, for now, needed something other than prognostic indicators. We stayed in this space for hours, feeling the anguish that stems from love. Darkness loomed, and I feared what death was trying to take from us.

I stepped into the hallway and Marielle, Ryan's nurse, stopped to ask how I was doing. "I'm sad," was all I could say.

She hugged me with tears in her eyes. "I'm sorry, Juli." She didn't try to minimize the situation with words. She couldn't fix it, but her presence was kind.

Years ago, one of my nursing professors told me, "Juli, with enough time and practice, you'll get the skills of nursing, but there are certain aspects of being a nurse, perhaps the most important ones, they cannot be taught. Compassionate care is what makes a nurse great."

Marielle was embodying these words in this moment.

As the sun was setting, our wonderful friends Sarah D. and Sarah O. stopped by the hospital to hug us and bring sandwiches and homemade Christmas cookies. As they stepped into Ryan's room wearing their gowns and masks, the nurse was changing Ryan's central line dressing. The weekly procedure was necessary but felt like torture each time.

The combination of pain and fear it elicited from Ryan ripped at my heartstrings. As she finished, I picked Ryan up to console him. He vomited all over my back and hands.

Sarah D. graciously lent me the red and white polka dot sweater she was wearing. At first, I didn't know that it was her late mom's sweater, one she wore months earlier while fighting her battle of cancer. The sweater still had one ondansetron, an anti-nausea medicine, in the pocket.

When I realized the significance of Sarah's sweater, I tried to take back my request to borrow it. Her response, "My mom would want you to wear it." And so, I put it on, wrapped up in a mother's love, and took another deep breath in.[20]

Ryan was back in Titus' arms. While the Sarahs were with us, Ryan perked up a bit for a few moments and surprisingly wanted to eat. He had not been willing for days, but he reached for the applesauce on the bedside table. Small bites were placed in his sore mouth with a tiny spoon. He ate and then used his limited energy to clap his hands.

Everything about the moment was laced with meaning. It was sacred, and as I sat and watched, I wondered whether the applesauce was Ryan's last supper or a gift telling us there was still life to come. I didn't know the answer but took in the moment and held it all.

Ryan spent the night resting on Titus' lap. It was his safe place, after all. There was love on display as Titus spoke tenderly to Ryan, "*Ami yu. Ami yu*, Ryan." I am here. I am here.

---

20 For months to come, I was convinced the sweater had been red with white hearts. To me, it was a palpable sign of being wrapped in love and community, and a fond memory from a shadowy day.

* * *

Day plus-11. "It's time for Ryan to move to the PICU," Dr. Federman broke the news. "His liver is failing, and it is going to get a lot worse before it might get better."

All I could do was nod. My red, tear-stained face knew what Dr. Federman said was true. His communication, especially the non-verbal parts, told me that he cared. As he prepared to leave Ryan's room, he said, "I know this isn't good news, but it really helps that he already has the dialysis catheter. He's going to need it—for dialysis."

Dr. Federman's words floated within my head as I took the nest apart, piece by piece. *It's going to get worse before it might get better.* The nest I had built to comfort and protect my child didn't work. My best attempt was not enough. *Did we really come this far for Ryan to die? Was the only option for a cure going to kill him instead?*

I could hardly catch my breath as I removed strands of Christmas lights and threw them into a blue duffle bag, along with the toddler-sized flannel pajamas. I grabbed the photographs of our children from the walls and stuffed toys into plastic hospital belonging bags. None of these items were of any value apart from Ryan, and suddenly, they all felt cruel.

Anger, masking my sadness and fear, overwhelmed me. I didn't know what to do with the stuff, where to store it while we moved Ryan to the PICU on the fifth floor. Considering everything, it should have been the least of my concerns, but it toppled me. I called Mel and Mary, "I don't know what to do with the stuff..." As I tried to get the words out, I began to weep.

Mel jumped in, "Don't worry, Juli, I'll come and get it." He made the hour-long drive to UCLA and packed up the car. He gave me a hug, then drove away.

* * *

"Juli, this is going to sound crazy," my long-time friend Mike emailed. "Is there any chance I saw Titus at UCLA? I could swear I saw him in the hospital cafeteria." Mike was a surgical resident but not at UCLA Medical Center. He had just been assigned to come over for a two-week clinical rotation. His stint overlapped with Ryan's time in the PICU.

Mike, whom we affectionately refer to by his Kalenjin name, Chesumei, was like a brother to me. We had shared many adventures and traipsed countless miles all over villages in East Africa. The following morning, Chesumei showed up in his surgical scrubs and hugged Titus and me.

Every morning and every evening and whenever possible in between, Chesumei came to visit Ryan. He cried alongside us, prayed over us, and made time to go to the cafeteria with Titus to share meals. His unexpected presence was like a security blanket.

Again, it was the kindness of God that allowed us to share the weight of Ryan's suffering. We were wandering in the darkness, and it was terrifying. But we were not alone. There were surprising reminders all around us.

* * *

Our nurse and an assistant maneuvered Ryan's bed through the animal-lined hallways. Ryan was propped up by pillows as it was nearly impossible for him to breathe or find any sort of relief while lying flat. He wore a Mickey Mouse-print surgical mask and a peach hospital gown.

I sat beside him in the bed, peering through the mesh sides encaging us. We made our way beyond the double doors, and the walls turned white and sterile. The beeping monitor sat at the foot of the bed with wires connecting leads onto Ryan's chest wall. IV tubing dangled from the ports in his chest. He didn't know where we were going—neither the place nor the reason.

Members of the PICU team were waiting to receive us. A new nurse introduced herself and removed Ryan from his fort. "He isn't stable enough to stay in there," she said kindly. "It isn't safe. In case we need to do resuscitation, it's important for us to have easier access to him."

She was right, I knew, but it seemed ironic. The fort wasn't safe.

She delivered more bad news. "Ryan's respiratory panel just came back showing he has two separate viruses: rhinovirus and adenovirus. The infectious disease doctor will be coming to talk to you about it. For now, the strict wearing of gowns, facemasks, and gloves will be required."

Again, I simply nodded.

She listed the PICU rules. While listening, it struck me how loud it was in this new space—white noise along with incessant beeping from monitors, IV pumps, and other machines. *It's really loud.* My brain was overstimulated and having trouble sorting through the clamor to focus on the nurse's words.

The front of the room and the sidewalls consisted mostly of glass with sliding doors. The back wall had a big picture window with a million-dollar view of the Getty Museum up on the hillside. Frat houses on the campus below us twinkled with Christmas lights.

I would have gladly given up the view to be in a different place.

"No food or drinks are allowed in the room. Bathrooms are outside the unit. One parent may stay overnight—they sleep in a chair with a blanket and pillow," she went on. It was information overload. "In case of emergency, you will be asked to step out of the unit. Our PICU team will be in charge of Ryan's care, but his other doctors will still be visiting."

The nurse was nice, as were the others who stepped into our new glass space, but it was cold and loud in here—technical, sterile, and alone—as it had to be.

* * *

"What time was the defibrotide given?" Dr. Bulut, the attending PICU physician, asked during morning rounds. She looked sternly at the resident presenting Ryan's case, and you could almost see her brain spinning in thought. Her presence filled the space.

The resident hesitated to reply. "He hasn't received it yet. We are struggling to get all the medicine and blood products he needs into him."

Dr. Bulut ordered, "It is the most important medicine, the main reason he is here. We have to figure this out." She wasn't shouting or belittling the others, but her tone and gaze were serious and laser-focused. There was a narrow window of time and space to try and save Ryan's liver and—ultimately—his life. "We need to add another line immediately," she commanded. The task was done within minutes of rounds being finished.

The entire PICU, starting with Dr. Bulut, the other doctors, the nurses, and the care partners were a team of brilliant and highly skilled women, many of whom were also mothers. They shared this wonderful ability to fight bravely for their patients while remembering to be human.

* * *

Titus looked at me with sadness in his eyes. He loved Ryan as much as any father had ever loved their son. We both did. *How were we going to survive this?* Words were few and hard to come by, but Titus broke the silence: "Juli, I'll stay tonight, go home. You need to sleep. Let me do nights with Ryan. It's better for you to be here during the day when the doctors come around."

"Okay." I nodded, knowing even now he was trying to protect me. His unwavering commitment to me and our kids held me even when we couldn't be in the same place.

We were trying to get through the physical and emotional exhaustion involved in witnessing your child suffer to the point of death. Best-case scenario, this was going to be a marathon, not a sprint. Mel drove Titus to UCLA each evening so he could stay with Ryan. I would go home to take a break, attempting to sleep for a few hours. Then at 6 a.m., Mel and I met back in the kitchen, and he chauffeured me to the hospital while it was still dark outside, before traffic became unmanageable.

I would spend the day with Ryan, meeting with various doctors who were helping to coordinate his care. We had the PICU team, transplant team, nephrology, infectious disease, and palliative care team all rounding each day. It helped that in meeting with the teams, I understood the medical language and the large-picture goals as well as the barriers we were up against.

I told Mel, "You don't have to do this every day. I can drive myself." It was hard to receive such generosity, to "suffer the kindness," as I once heard it described.

His consistent response? "Everyone is asking what they can do to help you. This is what I can do to make it a little easier for you. I'll meet you in the kitchen at six."

Mel had many other important things to do, but instead—or on top of those—he made hundreds of trips back and forth across crowded freeways. His openhandedness created a sort of rhythm that helped save us that December.

* * *

At 6 a.m., we met in the kitchen. I packed the exact same breakfast every morning: a chunk of cheese, a handful of raspberries, and a toasted Ozery Morning Round. I didn't know what the rest of the day would hold, but this food comforted me. It reminded me I was alive, even though much of me felt like I was drowning.

The morning air was brisk and dark as I stepped outside. It was an LA sort of cold—mid-50s—when we climbed into Mel's Tesla. The seat warmers were already at work as the automatic gate creaked open on its rails, and we reversed out of the driveway. "I'm glad we're not in Indiana," I'd say each morning. "I'm not sure Titus would have survived the winter."

Mel had a big plastic cup of hot tea he'd sip as we made our way. Mama Micah scolded him about drinking hot beverages out of plastic, but it seemed that some habits die hard. NPR accompanied us along the freeway, telling us news from around the world. Certain stories were too dark and depressing to listen to.

"Oh gosh," I said as they featured a story about sexual abuse happening to refugee children in Syria. "Please turn it off." The injustice needed to be highlighted—I embrace that—but my already traumatized mind couldn't handle another horror. I couldn't filter the information in a healthy way.

Some moments required pause, to lament the brokenness all around. To take a deep breath in—death won't always win—and a long exhale to remember that there's no immediate relief.

I knew full well that God cares about the suffering in this weary world, including Ryan.

* * *

"Juli, you need to continue with your paper chain," my mom lovingly prompted me as we sat next to the window in Ryan's room. "Keep adding slips of paper. Ryan isn't dead yet. His story isn't finished." As she said the words, tears welled up. Again. She cut the construction paper and added another link for me.

I looked out the window to try and stop the tears and noticed a group of middle-aged maintenance men in the courtyard below. They were doing a morning yoga session together. The whole scene was ridiculously out of place, only they were serious about their downward dog stretches and sun salutes.

"What is going on?" I wondered out loud. My mom began to giggle, and I joined her in laughter. We sat and stared out the window for the next fifteen minutes, the entertainment value priceless.

* * *

"We think the adenovirus is disseminated throughout Ryan's blood," the infectious disease doctor told me. "In a healthy child, adenovirus would present like a cold. But Ryan doesn't have an immune system. This is very dangerous for him. We are waiting to get lab results back from an outside lab but also trying to decide what medication to give. There aren't any great options."

Her words increased the anxiety I was already swimming in. Ryan's liver and kidneys were failing. He was struggling to breathe. And now an infection added to what already felt insurmountable.

We needed the best medicine had to offer, but I was not convinced science alone would be able to save our boy. I was afraid, anticipating the grief of what seemed to be coming our way. I imagined what we would do when Ryan stopped breathing, when his suffering ended, and we were still a million miles away from home.

I pleaded with God to save him, if for nothing else to protect Sharon from another loss, another death of one whom she loved. Just like Ryan's bones had been emptied of their marrow, my words, even with God, seemed hollow. I pleaded but lacked words to utter all that my heart contained.

I remembered a little boy at Kimbilio Hospice who asked one day if there would be a box in his size too. There's something about a small coffin that always knocks the wind out of me. I don't know who said that the smallest coffins are always the heaviest.

I didn't want one for Ryan.

Sarah D. wrote a message that day with words I could receive. It became a guide for me that grounded my spinning thoughts and my troubled heart as we navigated the very hard unknown in the valley of the shadow of death. Sarah wrote, "Juli, be careful not to get ahead of God." Her words—spoken from a place of love—grounded me.

* * *

Day plus-12. On Tuesday evening, I arrived at Mama Micah's house and hugged Ella, Geoffrey, and Sharon. I was exhausted but tried to read to Ella. I held her tight in my arms but fell asleep midsentence somewhere in the middle of the book. She woke me up, her hands on both sides of my face, "Mama, you have to finish the book." But my mind was done for the day. I slept in small bits.

"Titus," I texted sometime in the dark of the night, "you know how sick Ryan is, right?"

"I know. Could we ask some friends to fast and pray with us?" he responded from his chair in the PICU.

"Yes, who do you want to join us?" I was having trouble making even simple decisions.

"Uncle Mosh, Mama Kathy, Sarah, and Sarah." Within minutes, they all agreed to enter into this Advent season with us, fasting and praying on behalf of Ryan. Added to the thousands of others from our Living Room network crying out on his behalf, this became a trusted inner circle to help carry us through each day.

Day plus-13. Dr. Bulut broke the news to me, "It's time to begin dialysis. And it looks like Ryan will need to be intubated by the afternoon." Our boy was tired of breathing.

As Titus and I were switching spots that morning, Mel had told me, "Juli, know where the Ambu bag is in case he stops breathing and you need to be the first to respond." I had quietly nodded and held tightly onto Ryan as I knew I wouldn't be able to hold him once machines were breathing for him.

Don't get ahead of God, I reminded myself.

Dr. Federman rounded with the transplant team. He asked a simple question that felt altogether too big to answer, "How are you?"

With most, I simply responded, "I'm okay." With him, I paused before answering, "Dr. Federman, what would be an appropriate answer?"

He looked me in the eyes and kindly said, "Devastated."

With tears streaming down my face, "Yes, that is how I am today."

* * *

I followed Ryan's labs religiously on my phone. Hour by hour, the numbers came in and gave meaning to what we could already see with our eyes. It was all trending badly. Some of the numbers felt incompatible—or at least not sustainable—with life.

Don't get ahead of God, I had to keep reminding myself.

Dialysis started, and by the afternoon, as Dr. Bulut predicted, a team of nearly twenty doctors entered our glass space in the PICU. Chesumei also stopped by and stood beside me. I sat in bed with Ryan in my arms, the doctors' collective presence a visible reminder of the gravity of this stage we had reached.

There was a team from anesthesia. I needed to sign a consent form for the intubation. Ryan's renal doctors, the PICU team, the palliative care team, and the transplant team all gathered around looking at us. It was a *lot* of doctors. The group must have received an alert that Ryan's condition was deteriorating further, and they all came, showing up at the same time.

Some stood in the room, others spilled into the hallway. I imagine how terrified and overwhelmed I would have been if I wasn't a medical provider. I scanned the sea of faces, doctors showing up to fight on behalf of my little boy who had traveled the world to receive their care.

At the back of the group, I saw the transplant team doctors. They were ours—the ones we knew, the ones who knew us. Their presence, along with Chesumei's, made me feel less alone in the crowded room.

By evening, a machine was breathing for our baby. And as awful as it was, he seemed more peaceful. He looked small surrounded by the machines, the countless tubes coming from every part of his body.

* * *

I sat beside him, my mind drifting to the day I first met Ryan wrapped up in the pink blanket. He was all of three pounds, surviving against all odds. Each day, I was praying for him to grow just a little.

Nineteen months later, I found myself praying again—or maybe *still*. For another day. For healing. For another chance to hear him laugh. Fasting and praying, crying out to God to intervene. To once more do the impossible for Ryan.

15

Wordless Prayers

didn't know as I sat in the darkness what the outcome would be. I was convinced, though, of the deep love God had for our Ryan. If I knew anything to be true, it was that God's goodness had not changed nor was it dependent on whether Ryan lived or died.

But oh, I longed for life and healing.

My prayers lacked words. I felt utterly exposed and vulnerable. I sat in silence and wept. One day at a time was too long. Instead, I learned to live moment by moment—one foot in front of the other. All the while, I wondered if God could hear my cries when I was not saying any words.

Somewhere in the middle, I heard a voice within, "Juli, Ryan doesn't speak. Do you think I can't hear his cries? Do you think I cannot see him?"

I began to imagine what prayer looks like for a baby. In the first months or years of their life, they cannot say a word. On the night Ryan was born and no one knew to pray for him, what did God hear? What did God see? And now that thousands of people from all over the world were interceding on Ryan's behalf, did I believe God saw our little boy differently?

The answer, I knew, was unmistakably no.

Did that understanding minimize the need to pray? I don't think so.

Are the prayers of the righteous effective? Yes, and the God of mystery sees the orphans, widows, and the vulnerable. This included me.

* * *

Before babies know how to speak, they are developmentally learning trust versus mistrust. And this is where I found myself in the PICU, learning—maybe unlearning—what it looks like to trust God.

A dear friend asked me, "What is Jesus teaching you right now?" At that moment, the only way I could respond was, "I don't know. I don't think Ryan's suffering is for me to learn a lesson."

My heart didn't have space for that kind of theology. I didn't need my child's pain to be unnecessarily meaningful. Were there things to learn in the season? Without a doubt. But it mostly felt like this was a time to unlearn. To make room for the tension I couldn't easily make sense of rather than trying to eliminate it. To keep leaning in even when it hurt.

* * *

I didn't forget the pain—even when I slept. One night, I dreamed that Ryan's heart stopped beating, and he died. I watched the doctors and nurses do compressions on his small chest, but it didn't work.

I woke up from the night terror and could not differentiate whether it actually happened or not. I sat in the dark, afraid and alone, wondering if it was more than a dream.

I stumbled into the kitchen to meet Mel at 6 a.m., troubled by the night, when Ella came out of the room crying. It was still dark outside, and she crawled up into my arms. "Mama, there's an octopus in my room. It's trying to wrap all around me."

I was tired and unsure of how to respond, but also angry that it was coming after Ella too. I looked her in the eyes and firmly instructed, "Ella, go to your room and tell the octopus to go back to the ocean. It does not belong here."

"Okay, Mommy," she said. Brave and bold, Ella went to command the octopus.

Mel looked at me and said, "It seems we all have an octopus in our room."

I smiled, "And they all need to go back to where they belong."

* * *

Sitting in the PICU, I felt more clumsy than surefooted, but I also wondered if perhaps courage was simply about showing up when you were afraid.

It is like the time Ella wanted to take *maandazi*, a Kenyan version of a donut, to patients at Kimbilio Hospice on Valentine's Day. She said, "Mom, I want to tell the sick people they are loved too, but I'm a little bit afraid."

I assured her, "That is exactly what being brave is, Ella, choosing to love even when it's scary." What was it about being a mom that enabled me to see for her what I often miss for myself? I was placing one step in front of the other, sometimes staying still and facing the pain and fear. I didn't want death to win, but I also didn't want to give it the power to steal this moment—or any moments—that I still had left with Ryan.

My friend sent me a link to the podcast *On Being* and encouraged me to check out the interview with Father Greg Boyle. I was already a fan of his work, of his beautiful storytelling abilities.

I listened to the episode from the corner of Ryan's PICU room as I waited for the doctors to round. Ryan, sedated in the bed next to me, looked peaceful even with all the tubing and machinery attached to his small body. The room was dark, and the December sun was getting ready to rise once more.

Fr. Greg's words were an hour's worth of light and love, like a balm of salve to my wounds. He talked about God in ways that seemed less about religion and more like a friendship. And how *that* friendship had guided him through the hard. He said words like,

> "If you presume that God is compassionate loving-kindness, that all we're asked to do in the world is to be in the world who God is, [then] you're always trying to imitate the kind of God you believe in... And love is all there is, and love is all you are, and you want people to recognize the truth of who they are, that they're exactly what God had in mind when God made them."[21]

---

21 Greg Boyle, "The Calling of Delight: Gangs, Service, and Kinship," Interview by Krista Tippett, *On Being*, February 26, 2013, Audio, 17:32, onbeing.org/ programs/greg-boyle-the-calling-of-delight-gangs-service-and-kinship/

Toward the end of the podcast, Fr. Greg talked about a mantra he's begun to live by. As he described it, I breathed it in deeply. I skipped back to listen again, on repeat, to this message my heart needed to absorb.

> "Whenever the desert fathers and mothers would get absolutely despondent and didn't know how they were going to put one foot in front of the next, they had this mantra. And the mantra wasn't 'God,' and the word wasn't 'Jesus,' but the word was 'today.' And that's sort of the key. There's a play off-Broadway right now, called Now. Here. This. When I'm walking, or before a kid comes into my office, I always say, 'Now. Here. This. Now. Here. This' so that I'll be present and right here to the person in front of me."[22]

Now. Here. This. In that moment, I was hurting and afraid but also choosing to be present to the child before me, made in the image of God, whom I loved more than life itself. And to be present to the God who wasn't far away.

* * *

A fabric banner of hearts hung just over my head. It originated in a workshop in Kenya, handcrafted with beautiful kitenge material, and found its place in the window of Ryan's room. Friends from our church in Los Angeles had sent it over. Its presence served as a reminder to me of two worlds colliding and declaring that God had the whole world in His hands.

I began saying, "Love makes us brave." In truth, it also makes us tired, stretching us further than we thought possible. I was learning a kind of love that never gives up, never loses faith, is

---

22   Boyle, Audio, 33:12.

always hopeful, and endures through every circumstance. A kind of love that far exceeds my comprehension or ability, all the while graciously inviting me in.

Now. Here. This.

16

Puffin Friends

Day plus-18. I arrived at the hospital at my normal 6:30 a.m. call time, eight days into our PICU stint. Ryan's numbers were improving. The infectious disease doctors were amazed when the external lab results came back and the adenovirus did not show up in his blood. There was talk of when and how to stop dialysis and to wean him off the ventilator.

Titus and Mel stuck around to hear the morning report. A new attending doctor was on the case. Something was different on this day, though. There was alarm and new concerns. It was all around us. I could feel it in my gut.

"His blood pressure keeps bottoming out, even though we've increased the vasopressors," Ryan's nurse reported.

The fellow jumped in, "We've been trying to stabilize it all night."

"What's the differential?" the attending asked. I recognized the valuable teaching moment at hand. I've participated in these types of discussions in clinical settings so many times as a nurse, but now I was standing here as a mother. It was personal, and it all seemed cold and detached. I didn't want my son to be the case study. But this was a teaching hospital and learn we all would.

"He's septic or has internal bleeding," the resident said.

"Compartment syndrome."

"Good observations," the attending nodded in agreement.

I was nauseous. *Oh God, not again.* My thoughts were spiraling. I didn't want any of these diagnoses. None would end well. Utter darkness clouded my mind. Science was doing its best, but once more, it didn't feel like it was enough to save our boy.

Don't get ahead of God, I reminded myself again. Truthfully, the *Now. Here. This.* was unbearable.

Death seemed to be winning. We needed a miracle.

The team ushered me out of the PICU as they worked to stabilize Ryan. I took the elevator down to the street level and walked the paths around the UCLA campus. People were all around me, busy with their day-to-day activities, but I felt alone.

The sun warmed my face as I walked loops around the campus. The grass was still green, the flowers in bloom, even in December. Students were finishing finals to go home for winter break. I didn't know where I was going, but I was afraid if I stopped the end would come. Tears flowed gently down my cheeks.

I found my pastors, Tom and Albert, waiting in the lobby of the hospital. As much as I tried, I couldn't keep it together. Tom hugged me, and a dam of tears broke open.

Tom and Albert stood on each side, holding me up as we made our way back to the PICU. We put our hands on the soft white blanket laid across Ryan's dying body. Tubes stuck out from all parts of him. So many machines working in unison to try and keep him alive. We asked for life. I cried for it.

* * *

Day plus-19. A new red-and-yellow dump truck that apparently sang had been brought to Ryan's room by hospital volunteers. It sat on the shelf in the corner. To me, it was mostly a reminder that Ryan no longer played. I crawled into bed next to him.

I couldn't pick him up, but I whispered to Ryan as I touched his face. He was restless even with sedation, but in an instant, he went from restless to limp. He had dislodged the breathing tube. Now all the machines were alarming loudly as the monitor's numbers plummeted toward zero.

I called for help as he crashed. "He's coding," the nurse yelled.

The room flooded with a team of doctors and nurses working to resuscitate my boy. The dreaded red clock on the wall began to move. This time, it wasn't to celebrate life being poured into Ryan. Instead, it marked the minutes they were fighting to keep him alive.

I was ushered into the hallway, once more, and left to wander by myself for what felt like an eternity.

* * *

The hallways outside the PICU were lined with a gallery of photographs of puffins. These tiny penguin-like birds with colorful beaks surrounded me—swimming and flying, sitting on ice. Panoramic views of a colony of birds and close-ups of individuals.

Inside the locked double doors only a few feet away, my sweet nineteen-month-old boy lay in his PICU room next to a banner of Kenyan hearts and a paper chain with thirty colorful links while a medical team resuscitated his lifeless body.

As a majority of America was in the hustle and bustle of Christmas parties and wrapping presents, I stood in a hallway, in an almost child-like manner, escaping momentarily the horrors, the disappointment of death, to venture to the Arctic with the magical little clown-like birds.

A world was praying for Ryan, and I, as his mama, was pleading, mostly in my non-verbal season of prayer. On a slow repeat, the cycle of prayer included: *Jesus, breathe life. Please help. Oh, shit.*

All these prayers were desperate. All that remained within me were raw, honest pleadings to a God whom I knew to be good on behalf of a little boy whom I wanted to live.

My faith was less than perfect. My responses weren't well put together. But I stayed in a hallway with the puffins and waited. And prayed. Through the angst and pain, my heart remained open, even though it felt shattered.

I don't know how many minutes the red clock in Ryan's room read when it was stopped and a doctor came out to the hallway. It may have been twenty. Maybe it was an hour. I don't remember most of what she said. But Ryan was still alive, and they were giving him a chance to breathe on his own with oxygen support. She led me back into his room.

Gently, I crawled in bed beside him and wept. Ryan's tired brown eyes stared into mine. Some thirty days earlier, we moved into the hospital wanting healing to come, hoping it would be simpler than this. Here I lay beside my boy in the middle of a brutal and gut-wrenching fight.

Yes, love makes us brave, but it comes at a cost.

I wanted the pain for Ryan to be over, but there was no rushing through this deeply human experience.

Why couldn't it be me instead of him?

I felt crushing angst and anticipatory grief. I wondered how and why it all went wrong. The ending—or, God willing, just the middle—seemed to be entirely different than what we had hoped or imagined.

As I touched Ryan's swollen face, I saw fear in his eyes. I hated that traumas followed one another since the day of his birth. Maybe even before. He was merely nineteen months old.

When was it going to be enough?

Ryan spent his first five days in this world without food. I don't know whose arms held him and told him it would be okay.

When we admitted Ryan to the neonatal unit in Eldoret, he shared an incubator with two other preemies. And at six months old, when he was full of laughter and discovering the world, the excruciating physical pain of a cruel disease took over.

When was it going to be one too many?

The devastating reason why he hurt was for me to hold and grieve. He only knew the pain that unpredictably and frequently filled his body. The infections that threatened his life. But here we lay, side by side, Ryan with new, fragile bone marrow growing inside of him that no longer contained sickle cell disease. And yet, would he survive to experience the freedom?

We sat on the thin edge, and death wanted to take my beautiful boy. I lay beside him broken and wounded by the hard, hard journey. But he was still here. For this moment, he was breathing on his own. I hummed quietly a version of the old Christmas carol that had been singing to my soul:

Silent night, holy night
All is calm, all is bright
Round yon virgin mother and child
Holy infant so tender and mild
Sleep in heavenly peace
Sleep in heavenly peace[23]

---

23   Franz Xaver Gruber and Joseph Mohr, "Silent Night, Holy Night" (1818).

17

Paper Chain Links

This fragile season reminded me of Ryan's first days as a newborn. His premature frame was tiny and frail, and I was not sure whether he would survive.

Oh, I wanted him to live. When I fed him teaspoons of formula every hour and prayed he would be able to tolerate it, and sometimes he did. We worked diligently to keep him warm and protected from germs as much as possible.

Everything we knew to do for Ryan, we did, but many elements felt beyond our control. Daily, we celebrated weight gains, successful feedings, and wet and dirty diapers. And we prayed.

Here I was again, feeling those familiar emotions. There were little improvements from day to day that allowed me, once more, to feed my baby with a syringe, praying he would be able to digest formula. I rejoiced over normal body processes, like breathing, eating, and peeing, that were impossible for Ryan only a few days prior.

I brought out the little red-and-yellow dump truck from the corner for Ryan to see. My friend Kathy was standing beside me and supported Ryan's weak and somewhat floppy body to sit up. Tubes still extended out of him, and monitors beeped in surround sound.

When the truck sang in a mechanical voice, "I'm a powerful dump truck, making my way from here to there," there was a glimpse of light in Ryan's weary eyes. Ryan reached out his hand to grab an orange ball from Kathy. His movement was uncoordinated, but his intention clear. He wanted to play.

Kathy handed Ryan the plastic ball, and he placed it in the truck. The orange ball popped through the hole in the top of the truck as it continued to sing, "I'm a powerful dump truck." A little more light entered his eyes and face.

To play, it is said, is to heal. Ryan was demonstrating these words. Kathy and I cheered him on, affirming Ryan's play with a sense of awe and delight as if he were winning an event in the Olympics.

Day plus-24. On Christmas Eve, I stood at the window watching brilliant colors of orange and red fill the skyline as the sun set over Los Angeles. My baby was resting within my arms when he noticed the Christmas lights shining from the frat houses below. He finally broke his silence and whispered hoarsely, "Wow."

And for a moment, all was well. It seemed, perhaps, he shared a sense of the wonder I also felt deeply.

Now. Here. This.

* * *

Day plus-25. A stocking filled with new toys sat at the end of Ryan's hospital bed after Santa and Mrs. Claus had passed by. I was humbled by all that Advent held for us.

Christmas afternoon offered us the gift of being released from the PICU to return to our beloved third floor. As the nurse pushed us down the corridor, I sat beside our little king, grateful he lived to see Christmas.

"Miracles are a retelling in small letters of the very same story which is written across the whole world in letters too large for some of us to see," C.S. Lewis wrote.[24] This Christmas, I was a witness to the small letters.

I was not able to be home for Christmas, and the ones I loved were scattered around. But they were alive and well cared for, and that was all I could ask for this year.

Two videos arrived via text of my children singing "Jingle Bells." One showed Ella standing next to Sharon while they worked together on a puzzle. Some five hundred miles away from me in Redding, Ella sang "Jingle Bells" at the top of her lungs. Sharon looked unfazed, tolerating Ella's playful enthusiasm while she focused on the five hundred puzzle pieces in front of her.

The other video showed Geoffrey at the Herberts' house. Three months into our stay in America, the English language was being picked up like a sponge. Geoffrey proudly stood next to a Christmas tree he had painted and sang the same song—only his wonderful rendition was, "Jingle Mel. Jingle Mel…"

---

24 C.S. Lewis, *God in the Dock: Essays on Theology and Ethics* (Grand Rapids: William B. Eerdmans Publishing Company, 1970).

Oh, how much I missed sharing these moments with them, and how equally grateful I will always be for a community that was willing to fill in the gaps. The days and weeks that led to months of surviving through the kindness of others taught me, through practice, that community is more than an idealistic notion. It is people, like you and me, choosing to show up and love.

* * *

Each day, on repeat, I met Mel in the kitchen at 6 a.m. and grabbed my breakfast foods. There was no way to hurry the process—healing takes time. Ryan and I began to spend much of our days with him strapped to my chest in his purple Ergo baby carrier. He donned an argyle hat and Mickey Mouse facemask. We used hand sanitizer, all along the hallways, religiously, and avoided crowds.

I felt a new freedom in adventuring outside of the confines of Ryan's room. Pushing his IV pole with multiple pumps still connected to him, we rode the elevator up to the fifth floor. We walked back and forth along the hallway where we studied the long row of pictures containing my puffin friends. I read the captions to Ryan and marveled at the remarkable details surrounding these Arctic birds.

Ryan continued to say *wow* with astonishment. While on many levels, I was completely spent from the journey; I did not want to miss any of the healing we had been waiting for.

* * *

Titus and I saw each other only in passing for much of Ryan's hospitalization. He stayed at Ryan's bedside by night as I did by day. By the time we finally sat down together to share a meal at a

Thai restaurant, we had survived fifteen days of PICU and nearly another month of Ryan recovering in the hospital.

We were worn out. Grateful and traumatized. We laughed and cried and held on to one another that night. We were living the same story, but in many ways, doing it separately. We both knew it was required for this season.

During those dark months, Titus had quietly shown up, night after night, to sit at Ryan's bedside. To offer our son his courage and gentle strength. To protect Ryan and me by sacrificing sleep and taking on the night shift. His loving-kindness was a glimpse into Titus' unwavering commitment to our family. I missed him, though. And I had never loved him more.

Titus and Ryan

***

"Mel, how do you possibly say thank you to people who helped to save your child's life?" I asked as we drove along the freeway once again, the sun getting ready to rise.

"Write a letter," he said, "and give them a photograph. You just want them to know you're grateful."

So, that's what I did as we prepared to bring Ryan home. I wrote words on a card to say thank you to a whole host of nurses and doctors who had given their best on behalf of our son. It didn't feel like it was enough, but it's what we had to give.

***

Day plus-51. Sixty-one paper chain links filled Ryan's windowsill on the day we were finally told he could go home. As many days earlier, I had arrived in Westwood with the words *let the healing begin* resonating within my soul.

It had been fifty-one paper chain links since Sharon donated her bone marrow and Ryan received his transplant. Forty links since the hard letters of VOD appeared, followed by the equally hard letters of PICU. Thirty-eight chains ago, when almost everything was dark and uncertain, I wrote these words on a yellow strip of paper: *Don't get ahead of God. Stay present.*

While most links only had a number penned in black sharpie, a few pieces represented prayers from days when I had very few words to speak. Phrases like: *Please don't let him bleed. Let his kidneys work again. Small steps forward.*

Colored pieces of construction paper symbolized days of deep darkness but also moments of consummate kindness. Sixty-one links marked by mourning and dancing. Days when I wanted to stop adding links, and my mom lovingly reminded me the story wasn't over yet.

Sixty-one days made space for gratitude to grow within me, allowing an awareness of the seemingly ordinary gifts I never needed to take notice of before. Those days caused me to slow down and ponder many a thing.

While there were questions without answers and a whole mixture of emotions from moment to moment, I was humbled by the process. We found a safe place to land, where we were loved, even when we lost all control. The ups and downs were often extreme, but the kindness of God—so often on display through our community—was an indescribable gift.

* * *

The bags were packed when Mel and Titus walked into Ryan's room. With tears in his eyes, Mel leaned down toward Ryan and asked, "Ryan, are you ready to go home?" It was a question that even weeks ago was outlandish. Our minds did not have the space for this kind of possibility, for the hope that he would somehow live through the horror.

Ryan, wearing the navy beanie that had covered his bald head so much of the past sixty-one days, was ready to walk out in his new gray moccasins.

The nurses lined the hallway to give Ryan a get-well balloon and send us on our way. Their presence took me by surprise. This team, in doing their jobs, had lovingly walked alongside us over the past two months. Their knowledge and skill had given our son a new chance to live. In hard and then even harder times, the nursing team remained focused and kind, doing what needed to be done with a sense of unwavering commitment and care.

All I could manage to utter was, "What you do here is beautiful, thank you. We love you!"

The nurse educator replied, "What *you* do is beautiful! We are going to miss you!"

Never far from my mind was the unbelievable reality that we needed to do this again for Geoffrey in a matter of months. "Oh, we'll be back."

* * *

Mama Micah, Senge, and the kids were waiting outside to welcome us at home. The California sun shone warmly in January. In Sharon's handwriting, a banner painted in red letters read: Welcome home, Ryan!

In true Kenyan style, there was singing. And there were tears flowing as we all miraculously stood in one space again.

Time stopped for a moment as I looked around our little tribe. Love was here in plenty. The sacrifice required was immense and grueling. The anguish and devastation, the fear we endured was not erased. The trauma didn't evaporate, but rather, room was made for joy to find its way, intersecting the space.

For the first time in sixty-one days, our family was together under one roof again. Ryan moved back into his Pack 'n Play in the corner, and Titus lay in the bed beside me. I cut off the purple hospital wristband, the parents' admission pass, from my arm. I didn't need it tonight. I took a moment to write these words:

> I am grateful for breath, urine, and platelets. I am thankful for appetite and a tummy that can digest even a few ounces of formula again. I am grateful for medications that have helped sustain Ryan but also amazed on the days when he does not require all of them anymore.

I love the little gray moccasins that hold and protect Ryan's feet. There were days I didn't know if he would need shoes again. And now, as more and more life returns, he wants to dance. It makes my heart rejoice.

I am thankful for sleep. There were days and nights when Ryan could not, and the delirium was overwhelmingly scary.

I am in awe of the wonder that fills Ryan's spirit. He is causing me to say "Wow" a whole lot more than ever before. Oh, and his hugs and kisses. They are spontaneous and generous.

I love the "roar" sound Ryan makes when mimicking Simba, and his laughter is like medicine to my soul. The richness of it. The delight on his face, especially when he saw his brother and sisters. Oh, the gift it is to have them all under one roof.

I have observed friends posting #staylittle and #slowdown hashtags in reference to their kids. While I understand the sentiment, I am grateful for the possibility of my little one living to grow big.

As for the slowing down, I am convinced the responsibility for this is solely on me: I have to notice and receive these gifts, knowing that every good and perfect one of them is from above.

18

Side Effects

Ryan came home from the hospital on twenty-one different medications—basically, a whole pharmacy to procure, organize, and administer up to three times a day.

An entire section of Mama Micah's kitchen was now dedicated to bottles of medicine, syringes, and pill crushers. IV antibiotics were kept in the garage refrigerator, next to the wine. Mama Micah designed a two-page spreadsheet to guide the process of giving Ryan his medicine.

If you can, imagine the wrestling match involved in simply giving a teaspoon of Tylenol to a toddler. Now multiply this over and over again, day after day, for months on end.

Tacrolimus was one of the medications that accompanied us home, a necessary drug intended to reduce and prevent Ryan's risk of developing graft versus host disease (GvHD).

One possible complication of a transplant is that Sharon's donated cells would not recognize Ryan's body as its own, and the cells would begin to attack his body. GvHD ranges from a mild illness to a life-threatening disease.

The problem with the medication was how nearly impossible—at least in my limited experience—it was to get to a therapeutic dose. Each week, we returned to UCLA to draw Ryan's labs and measure the medication levels. If he got too little, he would be at increased risk of GvHD. Too much, and the side effects would be terrible. Basically, we spent months increasing and decreasing the dose but never finding a sweet spot.

One of the side effects of the medicine was that it causes the patient to lose magnesium. As a result, magnesium was supplemented to help avoid the side effects of tacrolimus. It was complex, but we did not want muscle cramps, seizures, heart arrhythmias, and other disastrous complications.

In Ryan's case, nine enormous pills of magnesium were crushed every day, divided into three doses, and mixed into yogurt. Thankfully, his taste buds had been killed by the chemo, so he was mostly agreeable.

I can still hear the sound of the twisting and grinding of those pills, though. As a bonus, a liquid form of magnesium was also given three times a day to accompany the horse pills.

For anyone who has ever taken Milk of Magnesia for constipation, you understand the predicament we found ourselves in. Magnesium is a laxative that causes rapid and frequent episodes of diarrhea. Ungodly amounts of poop.

With each weekly return visit to the doctor's office, they would ask, "How are Ryan's stools?" Too much poop could be a sign of GvHD, as well as simply a side effect of the obscene amounts of magnesium we were shoveling into him. The doctor would continue, "Is it normal?"

I laughed each time as there was absolutely nothing normal about this kind of poop.

We talked about frequency and volume and whether it was too much. Let's just say, I probably owe Mama Micah a new washing machine. After the months of magnesium, hers will never be the same again.

The day we started weaning Ryan off tacrolimus and were able to slowly reduce the amount of magnesium was one of the best days of my life—even if it did take months of weaning. Obviously, I was deeply grateful he didn't need the medicine any longer, meaning Ryan's body and Sharon's blood were coexisting nicely together. But we were all ready for a reprieve from the poop.

* * *

Ryan's IV medicine, found in the wine section, was infused twice a day through a pressurized ball-like pump, jerry-rigged with a paper clip to the back of his shirt.

As the home health nurse instructed me, "First, you start by washing your hands." Check. "And then gather your supplies—gloves, alcohol swabs, saline syringes to flush the line—and you infuse the antibiotic. When the infusion is complete, add heparin to make sure the line doesn't clot off." Check.

Most days, I relied on my nursing experience to guide the process, but there were mishaps along the way. "Where's the cap?" I'd ask broadly. Its absence meant Ryan's central line was no longer sterile.

"Ella, did you touch Ryan's line? You didn't eat the cap, right?" These types of conversations went on constantly.

Each such event required another trip to the emergency department. A master's in nursing helped prepare me for all of this, but I still felt inept most days. The complexity of coordinating medication pickup—*on which day? from which pharmacy?*—and determining when insurance would approve the next allotment for twenty-one separate medications was a full-time job.

We monitored Ryan's fragile body constantly, wanting him to be further ahead in the healing process than he was. And his big brother was still dealing with daily complications related to sickle cell disease along with the preparations involved in getting him ready for his transplant.

During those days, I often asked myself how other families managed this. I had been a nurse for sixteen years and was now living in a home with another nurse practitioner and physician, and it was still all-encompassing.

How do others survive?

Months—even years—of recovery and follow-up care was involved after a transplant. I knew this going into it, but now we were living the day-to-day realities.

* * *

Day plus-100 is a marker doctors use as an indicator for success. Any infection in the initial hundred-day period is risky to the graft and dangerous to the person. Every fever requires immediate readmission to the hospital.

Because of Ryan's vulnerability, we hid as a family at Mama Micah's home, restricting all movement and washing our hands religiously.

Senge kept Ryan tucked away in the back room whenever the high schoolers were around. She lovingly cared for him in that sun-filled space for hours at a time. Playing with toys. Reading books. Administering magnesium. Consuming Netflix. Changing diapers. Repeat and again.

* * *

We did all we could to create normalcy for our kids. To say we succeeded at that would be like saying Ryan's poop was normal. Far from it. It was all too much.

The girls weren't allowed to go to school as the flu season was in full effect. We couldn't take the risk of them getting it.

Mama H. came over several afternoons a week to tutor Sharon in math and reading and to play with our kids. Ella took a few dance classes at a nearby studio, and Sharon joined a running club. Not surprisingly, she was strong and fast. But mostly, Sharon poured herself into making art, finding a refuge within it to process loss, family, and home.

Grief is messy and unpredictable. Standing in the kitchen with Sharon, we were waiting for muffins to bake in the oven when she began to weep. Something triggered a memory of home. A memory of a mom who lovingly braided her hair and was no longer here. A baby brother who died one day while she was at school. She returned home that day to find he was no more.

I held her and spoke love over her, even though I knew it wasn't enough. It was all I had.

She experienced the vulnerability of being a girl in a village where poverty too often forces you to grow up faster than you should. The tension of feeling safe and having enough for a season in America and not knowing if the same was true for brothers and sisters on the other side of the world. The paradox of wanting what home offers and wasn't available in this world of plenty.

Learning to listen, to pay attention was heart work. And truthfully, my heart was spent. I wanted to love Sharon well but didn't always know how to do it.

I lacked energy and time, as several crises arose from one day to the next. Or simply another medication to give, another owie to attend to, another doctor to see.

* * *

"Juli, I don't think Sharon can hear out of her left ear. She keeps turning her head," Titus had mentioned several months earlier.

"Titus, are you serious? There can't be another thing wrong. We already have enough. She can hear," I said dismissively. But in between transplants, as I spent more time with Sharon, I began to wonder if Titus had been right.

I scheduled a doctor's appointment to check it out, embarrassed that I hadn't paid better attention or listened to the man who does it well. At the doctor's office, Sharon indeed failed her hearing test.

The doctor gave me three assignments to work on. "First, Sharon should see an audiologist. Second, you should try and have her see a grief counselor. And third, you need to talk to her about puberty."

I nodded my head. *Oh, is that all?* Wanting to both laugh and cry. I became a parent like two minutes ago. How did all this responsibility become mine?

It wasn't so much a complaint or unwillingness; I just wasn't ready. I am a rule-follower; I'd figure out how to get it done. But I had skipped over some important developmental stages in my journey of parenting.

One by one, though, we worked through the list. After a thorough examination and history by the audiologist, Sharon sat in a soundproof booth, headphones on. She grinned from ear to ear, even though she could hear exactly zero percent in her left ear. The technician turned to look at me, astounded, "She compensates really well."

"It seems so," I said, not expounding on the fact that I didn't even notice for months that she had a hearing deficit. We left the appointment with no interventions prescribed, just the awareness that Sharon couldn't hear—probably since birth—in her left ear.

Still amazed, I asked, "Sharon, you really can't hear anything from your ear?" She smiled, sipping a vanilla milkshake. "Why didn't you say anything?"

She shrugged, "It's always been like this. What would I say?"

* * *

We were recommended to a counselor named Susan, a trusted guide who could help Sharon begin the hard and important work of acknowledging and processing grief and loss. Susan met regularly with Sharon. She used a method of counseling that focused on resiliency and coping, not pushing Sharon to rehash all her traumas. Together they made space for emotions.

Susan encouraged Sharon to identify safe places within and around herself for when she felt overwhelmed or afraid. She gave her permission to experience joy and play, making room for Sharon to share whatever felt important to her.

In the short time we had been in America, it felt like Sharon went from being eight years old to thirteen in a matter of months. She grew and developed physically as well as experienced the emotional lability and hormonal changes that happen to every adolescent girl.

But she did it within a new culture and environment. Within a new family and during a time when her brothers were sick. In and out of the hospital. She searched for belonging while wanting freedom. Testing the reliability of relationships and boundaries. She was trying to find her way, and it wasn't always easy.

I was attempting to do the same, floundering along the way.

I sat beside her on a twin bed that had become hers and read books, word-for-word, about puberty, and then translated the cultural parts that she couldn't relate to.

"What if I don't want to have a period?"

"Well, then you will be in the same category as every other girl on this planet."

* * *

"Titus, do you think we're always going to be this tired?" I asked as we walked down the street to the grocery store. Emotionally and physically, I was spent. I gave all I had to give during Ryan's transplant. I knew Titus felt the same. But the journey wasn't over, not for Ryan's recovery.

I needed time and a sort of unhurriedness like I had never experienced before. My thoughts were fragmented. Simple decisions overwhelmed me. Multitasking—even though tons needed to be done—was entirely unavailable to me. And the crazy reality of what was still before us never left our minds.

We needed to jump back into the deep end and do it all over again for Geoffrey.

"Juli, I don't know if we should do the transplant for Geoffrey. I don't want to do it again."

Titus was missing home, and he was filled with an inner turmoil over what to do. We still knew, in our heads, moving forward with Geoffrey's transplant offered him the greatest chance to live; we also now understood, experientially, how close, even in a best-case scenario, it takes you to death.

We ached with how much we wanted life for him but also from how much it was going to cost to try and get it.

* * *

I found myself both tired and sleepless each night, wrestling within about what still lay ahead. Ryan, asleep in his Pack 'n Play in the corner of our room, was getting a little bit better day by day. Slowly, more and more life returned. It was new life, unhindered by sickle cell disease.

For months, we refused to say it out loud, but Ryan didn't have it anymore. His hair was still sparse, his skin discolored with blotchy patches and ever-changing rashes. His frame still fragile. And his eyes were constantly glazed from all the medications. He spoke almost no words. But he was alive and filled with the most beautiful sense of wonder. It took my breath away.

* * *

Days and weeks led to months by now, and we were becoming a family. Sharon and Geoffrey were no longer just Ryan's siblings, they were our children too. None of us really knew what it meant except that it was true.

The birth order of our children was messed up. Sharon was the oldest but not the firstborn; however, she was no longer willing to let Ella always win.

Ella, the firstborn, was no longer the oldest. She was okay with all the kids being in our family as long as she could still be in charge. Since that was no longer happening, she had a lot to say about the situation without much of a filter.

Geoffrey thought he was the baby but wasn't the youngest child.

And then there was Ryan, the youngest, who had spent so much time away from the others, he kind of functioned like an only child.

Add in the cultural differences, language barriers, drastically different lived experiences, multiple losses, and chronic illness. To say the least, we were complicated.

We were living ten thousand miles away from home with another family who had made space within their lives to welcome us for nearly seven months now. The guesthouse was still in limbo, and we weren't going anywhere anytime soon.

In all our complexity, with all the brokenness, in a beautiful and hard space, we learned more of what it looks like to love. And to be a family.

* * *

Two months after Ryan returned home, it was time to begin the process again for Geoffrey. Because he had been living with sickle cell disease longer and had been receiving blood transfusions since arriving in the US, his liver was at higher risk for developing the same complications Ryan had experienced.

In the weeks leading up to Geoffrey's hospital admission, the transplant team placed him on a medication to remove the excess iron from his body. Initially, he took the medicine by mouth, but the team decided another drug was necessary—a medication that would be infused each night through a needle into his belly, for fourteen consecutive days.

When I picked up the medication in a cooler box from the pharmacy, there were needles and tubing, and a portable pump that looked like it was from 1979. The nurse told me to use a nickel to open the lock on the back when the batteries needed changing.

I explained to Geoffrey how I needed to put a needle—just a little poke—into his belly to give him medicine. It would infuse overnight and stay connected while he slept.

Geoffrey looked at me with his sweet face and said, "Mama Ella, you're not going to shoot me, right? Mama Ella, you're not a doctor. You can't shoot me."

"Actually, Geoffrey, I need to give you the medicine."

He did not buy it, not even a little bit.

* * *

I wish I could have told my exhausted, spent, burnt-out self, sitting in the backseat of the car that day—terrified and anxious at the thought of yet another trip to the edge of death with yet another child I loved dearly—that everything was going to be alright. Not for months, but eventually. That Sharon's cells would intrinsically know where they were needed and find their way smoothly there. I wish there would have been the assurance that this was the right thing to do.

We knew too well that death was a part of any transplant journey, but on that Sunday afternoon we wanted to be certain that sickle cell would be the only thing to die. We wanted to know there wouldn't be any more rattling ventilators or infections that would threaten to steal our child.

It was too soon. Too scary. Too much. But we loaded up the car anyway, and Mel drove as I sat in between Titus and Geoffrey in the backseat.

Titus held my hand as I leaned my head against Geoffrey's car seat. We made our way back to UCLA. After all, this was Geoffrey's greatest chance at life.

19

G is for Geoffrey

"G is for Geoffrey," he repeated with delight over and again as his hospital bed went up and down with the push of a button. Leaning against his new Paw Patrol pillow where "Chase is on the case," he entered his own transplant adventure, the one where healing was supposed to come.

I didn't say that with entitlement but with hope along with residual trauma.

The last time I was in this room, some hundred-plus days ago, I was shoving Christmas lights and cozy toddler pajamas into a duffle bag while tears dripped from my face. I had sat on this same corner couch, tucked against a picture window overlooking the UCLA campus.

This was where—after the first twenty nights of Ryan's treatment—the dream of having a well child nearly died.

I was not ready to build another nest. I was not ready for what might be ahead of us, but here sat Geoffrey giggling as he played with his bed, soon calling it his airplane bed.

Geoffrey was three years old, maybe four. His birth certificate read Geoffrey Kiplagat, born on July 7, 2014. It was merely a piece of paper telling of a day—give or take a year—when the world became better because of a little boy named Geoffrey having been born.

And now he sat ten thousand miles away with a hospital bracelet to which he referred as his happy birthday bracelet. His enthusiasm was welcomed as I was struggling and didn't want to wear my purple, sharp-edged parent wristband again. As it was clasped on my left wrist, it felt like a familiar restraint with no end date in sight.

I first met Geoffrey, along with his other brothers and sisters, a few days after Ryan was born. Sitting in a line outside their mud house, he was the littlest.

An uncle explained on that day that "Something seems to be wrong with Geoffrey." Some six months later, we got a diagnosis, and the puzzle pieces finally started to fit together.

His "broken foot" which caused him to fall incessantly was the result of a stroke.

People often asked me when it happened, and I almost always said, "When he was two." The truth is, I don't know. It was some time before I met him sitting on that hillside, where his mama's grave was all I could see in the background. And it was some time before his falling had any meaning to his family.

The amazing thing was—Geoffrey didn't seem to notice. Yes, he fell and cried and said, "Mama Ella, I fall down." But then after one of our crew—most often Mama Micah—picked him up and reassured him, he was back up and trying to run again. Kind of like Sharon's hearing impairment, he didn't know anything different.

He wanted to keep up with Ella and said, "See, I the fastest."

And she didn't dwell on his limitations either. Ella wanted Geoffrey to run with her, and sometimes she held his hand to help him out.

Other times, she only wanted to compete with him to win.

* * *

Shortly after receiving Geoffrey's sickle cell diagnosis, he was terribly sick. I held his little body in a waiting room in a hospital in Eldoret when he was still living at home with his oldest sister Jerono and with Alice.

We barely knew one another, but I loved his baby brother and wanted life for him. I kissed his cheek, and with no hesitation, he lifted his head to kiss mine. His affection surprised me that night.

Over time, I came to know it as one of the many beautiful pieces of this little boy.

Geoffrey wore his emotions on his sleeve. If he was happy, you knew. When he was sad, you knew. When he was hurting, which he often was, you also knew it.

A large stockpile of Band-Aids—or "bandages" as he termed them—was required to try and cover the hurt that was hard to treat and control. In the months leading up to his transplant, Geoffrey not only learned to speak English but developed greatly in his ability to articulate his emotions.

As mamas do, I often told my kids, "Use your words." But in truth, Geoffrey did well, saying, "That makes me sad" or "Mama Ella, it is hurting."

And now that we were in the hospital for the transplant, he was using his words: "I want to go home" and "I don't like that."

When the doctor came in to ask, "May I listen to your heart?" Geoffrey politely declined, "No, thanks."

His words—and often his lack of choice—were teaching me what it means to parent and support a child through a traumatic illness. As he led the way, I began to advocate on his behalf, telling the doctors and the staff, "If he does *not* have a choice, please don't ask him as if he has one."

* * *

While I encouraged Geoffrey and all my kids to use their words, I struggled to find my own. I was entering back into the darkness, and I didn't want to go there. Like a scared child going to the doctor's office for a shot, I knew what was coming and felt afraid; I wanted to scream and kick in resistance long before the needle came out.

I didn't want the long, scary corridor, the pain and suffering, the valley of death. I wanted the healing to come now, not on the other side of the hard. I wanted an easier, safer path. But on the day we moved Geoffrey into Room 3525, I was quietly wrestling from within, aware that the hardest thing and the right thing, in this moment, seemed to be one and the same.

No words could fully explain it or make it easier to embrace, but here we were. Again.

While I longed for the healing to begin, I was not ready to make another paper chain to count the days. I wanted to protect Geoffrey, but I couldn't build a nest in the same way.

This needed to be a journey of its own.

* * *

Time slowed down once more to teach me what it means to be like a child. I entered into the words of Mr. Rogers, when he said, "You were a child once too." To imagine without filters. To make new friends.

In Room 3525, Geoffrey was inviting me there too. To express emotions boldly: *I am afraid. I am sad. I am happy you are here. I want to hold your hand.*

Geoffrey often voyaged on adventures as chemotherapy infused into his blood. The IV lines that tied him to beeping medicine pumps didn't seem to bother or hinder him. He played around them while the rest of us dealt with the pulling and the tangling of the tubing. Whenever possible, Geoffrey escaped to his own world. One with rockets and dinosaurs, sailboats and parades.

He stood next to Mama Micah on the colorful floor mat by his airplane bed. Tiny animals marched and hopped, dialoguing about what to eat for supper or where their brother or sister were sleeping.

Mama Micah grabbed tightly onto Geoffrey's pajama pants with one hand, helping to steady him, while a blue cone was held up to her eye. Geoffrey's telescope cone was yellow like the sunshine, his new favorite color. They searched for rockets and stars, lands far away where things like sickle cell couldn't harm or reach them.

Geoffrey took a break from playing to "choke"—his word for vomiting—before returning to his magical world where all was well.

He tired quickly, and we helped him back into the green tented bed that goes up and down, maneuvering the IV pole with spaghetti-like tubes connecting to Geoffrey's chest. Geoffrey asked for Mama Micah to lay beside him as he drifted off to sleep while watching a show on the iPad.

* * *

Days and nights became confusing for Geoffrey, staying only inside, in one space, twenty-four hours a day. We opened the curtains to let the sunlight in, but the warmth of its rays and the freshness of outside air were absent from the room.

We wrestled to keep any sense of normalcy in a room where the primary goal was to keep Geoffrey alive.

Interruptions came at all times, day and night, from various members of Geoffrey's care team. Every vital sign was recorded on the nurses' computers except for one: rest.

How many hours of uninterrupted sleep was Geoffrey having? How was his sleep—or lack of it—affecting his physical healing? His and our emotional well-being?

The path we trudged was exhausting and the one ahead I knew only to be daunting. When Ryan's body was shutting down, the sense of threat I felt left me in a prolonged fight-or-flight response, hyperaware and feeling panicked, not for a day or week but months on end.

With Geoffrey, my stress hormones were already used up. My body couldn't feel at the same intense level. It was not because I didn't care. I cared deeply, but my body and emotional state were depleted, and giving in to a sense of numbness became my way of coping.

I showed up, committed to what was required but only parts of me were still available.

Now. Here. This.

The mantra remained within me.

* * *

A little boy needed me more than ever before, not to be Mama Ella but simply to become Mama. This seemingly subtle shift was monumental in our evolving relationship and within my identity.

He needed my lap to hold him. My voice to tell him it was going to be okay, even if I was not convinced. My encouragement to eat a few bites, to take his medicine. My hands to hold the plastic bucket when the choking wouldn't stop. He needed me to be present.

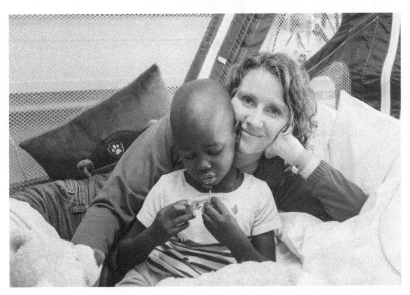

Geoffrey

"Will you sleep next to me?" he asked.

As I crawled into the airplane bed and lay next to Geoffrey, I spoke his love language. He giggled with delight as chemotherapy continued to run through his veins. He wanted to go home but rested contently for the moment with me beside him.

It undid me, expanding my heart, breathing life into my tired bones, into my weary soul.

How did I get this privilege that was both hard and holy?

I didn't ever knowingly volunteer to sign up for all of this, and yet here I was drinking in the joy and pain of this little boy.

It made me think again about his mother—the one who grew him, birthed him, and nursed him. I only knew of her through the lives of her children, but I wished I could sit with her over a cup of chai and understand more of who she was. To learn the details of each of these little ones I was coming to know as my own.

I wanted to hear the story of Geoffrey's birth, when he started to crawl, walk, and speak.

There were gaps in my knowing, but time taught me the tenderness of his heart. I learned to marvel at the richness of his laughter, the depths of his cries, and the warmth of his hugs.

While his short life, in too many ways, was marked by suffering and loss, Geoffrey was tremendously resilient, loving, and kind.

* * *

As Geoffrey went to sleep in the hospital at night, he prayed one ongoing request. It started sometime in the middle of the chemo treatment, his words whispered alongside the humming of IV pumps, "God, heal Alice."

It caught me off guard. We hadn't been talking about his sister's sickness, but it was somehow within him. His plea added space within my heart.

Is it possible that God will make a way for her too?

I lay beside Geoffrey, squished against the mesh lining of the bed, and I wanted the same life and healing for him, the kind he was also asking for his sister. The new life that now belonged to Ryan.

I desperately desired for the path taking us there to be smoother, but I was also learning—whether I liked it or not—new life begins in the dark.

* * *

When I moved to the village of Kipkaren, it was years before electricity would come. We used the sun by day and the moon and lanterns by night. One evening, a man in the community was having an asthma attack.

In the black of night, David Tarus walked with me to the man's home. This was before smartphones afforded us a flashlight in everyone's pocket. There were also no streetlights to guide us.

I could not see a thing, and David kept saying, "Step here," as I stumbled across a stream.

"I don't know where you are pointing," I would object. I was afraid and uncertain of my footing. But David couldn't understand why I could not see. He grew up without artificial light, so his eyes—like those of all our other neighbors—had adapted to see in the dark. He did not require a streetlight or flashlight to guide him.

As Geoffrey's chemo continued to run through his veins, it was like I was trying to cross that stream again. I couldn't find my footing, and my vision had not acclimated.

Yes, I had walked this path with Ryan, but here we were again, hoping the darkness was not the end for Geoffrey, hoping as Geoffrey's bone marrow died, it wouldn't kill him. Rather, new life would still come forth.

Barbara Brown Taylor writes, "Whether it is a seed, a baby in the womb, or Jesus in the tomb, it starts in the dark."[25]

I was learning that gestation cannot be hurried. It would take time, requiring a sort of waiting and aching I had come to know as hope.

* * *

Just as there was a happy birthday sign for Ryan's transplant, one was coming for Geoffrey. Sharon's bone marrow was frozen and waiting for the conditioning period to be completed.

Three days before Geoffrey's transplant, Sharon came to visit Geoffrey one last time. I was flying her and Ella up to Sacramento the following morning—which also happened to be Ryan's second birthday—to be with my parents. The girls would stay with them again until Geoffrey was well enough to come home, for as long as that might be.

So much was happening at once. The suffering of Geoffrey. The celebration of Ryan's remarkable two years. A difficult good-bye, once again, to our girls. My heart was a mess, trying to juggle it all. And community was carrying us in loving and tangible ways, every second of every day.

Sharon was wearing a sparkly gold paper crown—a remnant from Ryan's birthday party— when she entered Geoffrey's room. With a similar tenderness of 138 days earlier when she climbed into the hospital bed with Ryan, she did the same for Geoffrey and gave him the crown off her head. He smiled at her as she placed it on his head, now patchy from the chemotherapy causing his hair to fall out.

---

25   Barbara Brown Taylor, *Learning to Walk in the Dark* (New York: Harper Collins, 2015), 129.

Sharon sat beside him, offering her brother her full attention in ways they both needed, even if for a few moments. It was another glimpse of love.

* * *

On the afternoon of April 5, 2018, Sharon's bone marrow was brought into Geoffrey's room in a large stainless-steel canister. When it opened, a strange smell, something like creamed corn, filled the room. The same doctors who stood with Ryan four months earlier were with us again at the bedside of Geoffrey as the red clock on the wall started to run. Geoffrey was still wearing Sharon's gold crown as her bone marrow flowed through his veins.

Titus, Mama and Baba Micah, and I looked on. We were nervous, bruised, and battered from the long journey but still humbly aware of the sacrifice required for this chance at new life to be possible.

As the last drops infused, the red clock stopped, and the next phase of waiting began. We knew it well. Geoffrey had no immune system left, and Sharon's cells had the important work of finding their way to Geoffrey's marrow and making it their home.

All along the way, my point of reference for Geoffrey's transplant was Ryan's experience. In my head, I knew it could be different. Oh, I hoped it would be. But my mind and body, my emotions and spirit held the pain and fear. I read it like a datebook with every post-transplant day having a set of memories.

I knew where we were with Ryan as I looked at Geoffrey's lab reports. I could feel, with every fiber of my being, where we were on day plus-9 when Ryan's liver began to fail. Day plus-11 when we found our way to the PICU. Day plus-13 when dialysis and intubation came.

Part of our remembering was anchored in desperately wanting to make it through those days without repeating the same story. I held my breath as I opened lab reports each morning with a sense of relief. Geoffrey's labs were holding steady.

I acknowledged the miracle of watching his white blood cell count slowly rise a little each day from zero. The graft of Sharon's cells was in its infancy, fragile, but it was taking.

I texted the daily report to Baba and Mama Micah. A sign on Mama Micah's refrigerator door read in black and red marker: ANC 350 and then crossed off to read 480, followed by 740 and then 910.

We all followed with bated breath as his red blood cells and even platelets increased. At the bottom of the sign, it read: Go Geoffrey! Go Sharon!

* * *

Day plus-19. Geoffrey didn't sleep well again. He was vomiting, even though there was nothing in his stomach to vomit. And the diarrhea, it just wouldn't stop. The doctors thought it was GvHD and started him on high doses of steroids.

"I am not going to get better," Geoffrey said as tears streamed down his little face. My reply, as they also flooded my own, "*Pole*, Geoffrey. I am sorry. But you are going to get better." This was said less as a promise and more from hope and a prayer. "I love you, Geoffrey," I said these words on repeat to a little boy overwhelmed by his suffering.

Relief was a world away. "I love you so much, Geoffrey." As he sat on my lap or asked me to sleep next to him. As he refused to eat or drink anything for yet another day. When he needed to "choke" or the diarrhea wouldn't stop. When he was afraid. When I felt afraid. "I love you so much."

There were many things I did not know, could not control, or was unable to fix. Oh, but of this I was certain: I loved this little boy.

* * *

Ryan had taught me over the past few months more about what it looks like to live with wonder, and wonder I did in the moments of reprieve when Geoffrey found the strength to get out of his bed and play. He climbed back onto his bicycle and planned a parade. How he even had a concept of a parade, I didn't know, but it was a marvel to behold.

Geoffrey insisted that Teddy, Raccoon, and Hopper, three of his stuffed animals, be a part of the festivities. They were seated tightly in the bike basket. The Mother's Day balloon—a gift from the child-life team—was a wonderful kite used to carry us along. I had the privilege of trying to keep up with the IV lines while pushing all the pumps.

The bike transformed into a Tesla car that had to be plugged in and charged to keep us going through the mountains. Just like Baba and Mama Micah's.

In a blink of an eye, the white Tesla changed into a sailboat and the primary-colored striped hospital mat next to his airplane bed were the high seas. We battled through the ocean to find our way to safety, looking for home. Teddy, Raccoon, and Hopper helped all along the way.

With another blink, we were in a rocket with a booster, flying with fury to the moon. An adventure of a lifetime, and we had to hold on tight. We didn't want to miss a moment. Everyone, especially the stuffed animals, required their safety belts securely fastened around their laps, helmets on. And away we would go!

If I knew how to capture the magic of Geoffrey's play, it would be among the most beautiful stories ever to be told. In the middle of the dark, his play was breathing life back into both of us.

* * *

Day plus-39. After fifty days and nights in the hospital, Geoffrey was discharged to go home to Mama Micah's. It was the place, at this point, where he knew home to be.

For fifty days, with very little exception, Geoffrey remained within the confines of four walls. There was a window to show him when it was day and night. There was a door that opened and closed as the medical team entered and left.

But Geoffrey never went beyond it. For many weeks, he did not ask to go outside of his room.

His imagination, like Buzz Lightyear, took us to infinity and beyond! His play was hopeful and bold.

* * *

The work of healing was slow and hard. It was exhausting and grueling. The further we had ventured, the more I realized the "new life" was, thankfully, not only for the boys. I sensed pieces of myself evolving. Parts died while others came to life.

I no longer just tried to get through the pain or the treatment of this season. I started learning to notice simple things in the dark. Learning to be gracious with myself.

On one occasion—after another all-nighter at the hospital—I came home and took a short nap. When I woke up, I knew there were many tasks to do for Living Room, and I thought, *I am so lazy.* After a brief pause, I corrected myself. *I'm not lazy. I am exhausted.*

We were *all* exhausted. In many ways, our whole family—
along with the Herberts—was coming out of months of darkness.
We all needed to be tender with one another, with ourselves.

"Have patience. Don't be in such a hurry." I needed these
reminders more than a few times as an opportunity to grow in
trust and love.

This prayer by Teilhard de Chardin tells much of what was
held within my heart:

> Above all, trust in the slow work of God.
> We are quite naturally impatient in everything
> to reach the end without delay.
> We should like to skip the intermediate stages.
> We are impatient of being on the way to something
> unknown, something new.
> [...]
> Only God could say what this new spirit
> gradually forming within you will be.
> Give Our Lord the benefit of believing
> that his hand is leading you,
> and accept the anxiety of feeling yourself
> in suspense and incomplete.[26]

---

26   Teilhard de Chardin, "Patient Trust," in *Hearts on Fire: Praying with Jesuits*, ed.
Michael Harter (Chicago: Jesuit Way, 1995).

20

Life Lived Separately

On the day Geoffrey got to go home, Mel and Titus came to UCLA with Ryan for an early morning follow-up appointment. Titus was with Ryan getting his infusion while Mel carried our belongings to the car.

I waited to tell Geoffrey we were going home until the discharge orders were completed. I wanted to make sure there were no glitches holding us in the hospital. Once I knew, I asked him, "Geoffrey, do you want to go home?"

"Yes, to Mama Micah's house," he said, not looking away from his show on the iPad.

"Okay, let's go home." The news finally registered, and he smiled from ear to ear as I put on a Mickey Mouse surgical mask. One for him and one for me.

Holding him in my arms, we crossed the threshold from his room into the hallway and made our way into the unknown. There was no longer a barrier keeping us in a single space. Geoffrey was fragile, but we were going to Mama Micah's. His safe place.

Like his brother, Geoffrey no longer had sickle cell disease. Part of him died in that room while another was trying to find new life.

* * *

Much tenderness was needed each step of the way. Geoffrey's senses were easily overstimulated. He had endured the constant beeping of IV pumps, interrupted sleep, and suffering. Even small, distant noises were too loud, and he would plug his ears in disdain. The lights were too bright. He would cover his eyes and ask to make it dark.

We arrived at Mel's car in the parking garage, such a familiar space, but Geoffrey hadn't seen it for the last fifty days. We had to wait in the car for Ryan to finish his infusion. Baba Micah told him, "We're going to leave very soon. We need to wait for Ryan."

Geoffrey's response—without hesitation—was to sing, "Have patience, don't be in such a hurry."

When Titus arrived, Ryan's face lit up at the sight of Geoffrey. Brothers reunited, having such shared suffering and now healing. They sat side by side as we made our way over the 405 and into the valley where Mama Micah and Senge waited with a bouquet of colorful balloons and a sign that read: We love you, Geoffrey!

* * *

I flew to Sacramento days after Geoffrey came home from the hospital to bring Ella and Sharon back to Los Angeles. While they were in Redding, the girls were loved well and cared for diligently. There's no one I would trust more with our girls than my parents.

Ella and Sharon had attended school at my parents' church, creating a daily routine and the opportunity to learn and play. Redding was good to them, but it was another span of time where our ever-evolving family was not together. We weren't in the same space, doing daily life, and we missed one another. The separation created apprehension and unease within us all.

On the evening the high schoolers welcomed the girls back to Mama Micah's home, there was singing and flowers. It was a taste of what it's like to be welcomed in Kenya, even if they had never been there. The girls slid back into playing with their brothers, reading books on the laps of their high school friends.

I was able to breathe in and exhale in a way I hadn't for almost two months.

Micah and the other seniors were days away from their high school graduation. We cheered for them, proud of their accomplishments, and weren't quite ready to be done with their daily hangouts. The way our paths overlapped was an indescribable gift to our family. There were transitions happening for them that we got to witness, becoming a part of each other's stories in the most unlikely of ways.

* * *

The work of medication administration doubled when Geoffrey came home. Under one roof, we cared for two little post-transplant boys. We did all we could to protect their fragile grafts, to keep them alive and sickle cell free.

Geoffrey's pharmacy included the same medications Ryan was taking, with a few additional antibiotics and high-dose steroids. The garage refrigerator overflowed with IV medications to administer.

Geoffrey came home with his central line hanging from his chest wall. Thankfully, Hopper—the stuffed animal—came with one too. Ella played with Hopper, trying to understand all that was going on with Geoffrey.

Central line dressing changes were as painful and scary for him as they were for Ryan. We tried all forms of distraction to lessen how brutal they felt, as they still had to be done at least once a week. For the next few months, Geoffrey still needed his line, and we couldn't risk any infections.

* * *

Coming home and being with others was what Geoffrey wanted, but it also took time for him to adjust. For two months, Geoffrey had stayed in his one hospital room, and in many ways, his personality and behavioral patterns were altered by his time spent there. He didn't have words for most of it. They'd been sucked up by the hard, and we all felt it.

He was trying to find his way out of the darkness and back toward life. We all were.

The steroids caused his emotions and mood to be labile, and his appetite was ferocious. Geoffrey's face and body were taut and stretched like a balloon. In this tenuous time, we did a lot of dividing and conquering, without really talking about it.

Mama Micah spent countless hours with Geoffrey on her lap—reading books, playing with dinosaurs. Senge and Titus stayed occupied with Ryan. And I tried to help Ella process her many questions and concerns. Bedtime was especially hard as each child needed reminders that they were loved and were going to eventually be alright.

It took a highly devoted team to make it through each day. Micah jumped in to play with the kids and helped wherever needed. He built many a train track for Thomas and Percy to ride on. And Mel constantly walked to what he dubbed "the second kitchen"—the grocery store across the street—to pick up another gallon of milk or loaf of bread. On many afternoons, Mama H. stopped by with her little basket of tricks, activities to enjoy together. Books to read. Worlds to explore through imagination. There were other players too, selfless ones who kept showing up and giving of themselves in ways that blew me away.

* * *

Mama Micah's backyard pool created space for Ella and Sharon to learn how to swim, to jump into the deep end and experience the joy of water.

During that time, Ella's mission became to save bees from drowning in the pool. Each afternoon, while swimming, she'd line up the bees on the cement, calling it her bee hospital. I tried to warn her of the dangers, but she was adamant.

It wouldn't take long before she reported, "I met a mean one, and now my mouth is crooked." Her upper lip was massive, covered by a Band-Aid.

What upset her the most, though, was that the bee—the one she had been trying to save—would die because it lost its stinger.

Baba Ella sat poolside, and Ryan would join in after waking from his four-hour afternoon naps. His body required enormous amounts of rest each day. Ryan was still pretty much non-verbal, though he could follow instructions, and we often interpreted what it was he wanted or needed.

I worried whether the words would ever come, but Mama Micah encouraged me to give him more time.

* * *

Geoffrey's central line kept him from being able to swim much of the summer. He would, at times, sit poolside and kick his feet in the water. But mostly, he chose to stay inside.

He sheltered in place to keep cool and to cope.

Like Ryan, Geoffrey was sent home on IV antibiotics that were hung twice a day, and we opted to give his magnesium by IV overnight to avoid the crazy side effects. I wasn't ready—none of us were—for the explosive diarrhea from magnesium again. It had plagued Ryan, and I just couldn't do it. Not if there was another option.

There were mornings Ella and Geoffrey woke up and walked out of the bedroom before the infusion was complete. Ella slowly led Geoffrey while she carried the IV pump in her hand, the tubing still connected to his chest. It was two little ones waking up for a new day, a picture of what our lives looked like.

Their resiliency, even if fragile, was remarkable. They were children who wanted to play and share adventures, but there was also the trauma of disease and treatment, the anxiety of separation all around.

There were moments, hours, even days, when chaos and total meltdown filled the Herberts' house. We weren't temporary visitors anymore—there were zero small footprints.

We were all doing the best we knew to do, even if it felt like that wasn't enough.

Ten of us filled every corner of the house. We were nine months in, all working toward the same goal of two little boys being cured of sickle cell. It was a full-time, unpredictable sort of life that required all hands on deck, as Mama Micah always said.

Hundreds of books were read on laps that weren't mine. Art projects and field trips that were delightful and exactly what was needed, and I didn't participate in them.

I can't tell you what Geoffrey's days looked like while Ryan was in the PICU. I don't know who gave him a bath or all the pictures he colored. In the same way, I can't tell you what Ryan ate for breakfast on the day Geoffrey had his transplant.

I missed those moments while living others.

When Ryan fell and split his head open, requiring Mel to glue his forehead shut and make a trip to the ER, I was not present to hold him as I was with Geoffrey in the hospital.

Countless nights I went to bed while Sharon watched a show on Netflix, the only time she didn't have to watch cartoons with the littles. Too tired to stay up, I missed that experience with her.

And I missed Micah's birthday party.

Senge was this quiet, often behind-the-scenes figure who filled in gaps all along the way. Yes, she may have wanted to "get off the bus" on more days than one, but she didn't. She stayed in the middle of the hard. She spent countless hours with Geoffrey while Ryan was in the hospital and then switched kids, helping Ryan to recover. She stepped in for a day here and a night there on the third floor of UCLA, giving Titus or me a break to go home.

The girls spent months at my parents' home. I don't know all they felt, what they ate for breakfast, or what letters Ella learned while she attended preschool in Redding.

It was a shared journey that cost everything we had to give, but none of the ten of us lived it all together. For a year, we spent Halloween, Thanksgiving, Christmas, New Years, Mother's Day, Father's Day, and most birthdays in the hospital.

We each walked our own story within a larger story unfolding before us. Together, we dared to dream of life for little boys that would be disease-free.

We were learning collectively how to say yes to what was before us—trusting, leaning in, and letting go. We were marked permanently by the suffering and the healing, but none of us lived it the same way.

For any of it to be possible, we were forced to take shifts, filling in gaps as needed, adjusting plans, giving up on timelines, holding on tight for the craziest ride imaginable.

We checked in with each other constantly, shifting roles when needed, reporting from the home front, the hospital, my parents' home in Redding.

It isn't possible to quantify how much it cost—emotionally, financially, or timewise. It's hard to measure how much it altered Micah's senior year of high school to share his bathroom with toddlers and his parents with the unpredictable patterns of all that our family brought with us.

There were no days off as we fought to keep children alive. There were always medications to give, IV antibiotics to administer, prescriptions to refill, books to read, laundry to fold, dishes to wash, schools to choose.

There were also diapers and central line dressings to change—though not at the same time, of course. And there were medical appointments, hospitalizations, unexpected fevers, and ER visits.

We were all plugging holes, living a profound, life-shaping journey alongside one another but each having our own lived experience. Of the thousands of photographs from our time at Mama Micah's, almost none have all ten of us in them.

So much life was being lived separately.

21

Firestorm

O n graduation day, I didn't realize how school closing would leave a gaping hole for our kids. We were used to the high schoolers' constant coming and going, their eagerness to play, willingness to do a puzzle or blow bubbles.

When school finished and they stopped coming over, the trauma of the last year began to catch up with us. Pieces of us started to crumble.

By early July, about the time of Geoffrey's fourth birthday, Senge chose to go back home. She had given selflessly and carried us for months, but she was ready for a change.

I will always be grateful she chose to journey with us through some of the darkest of times. Her constant love and presence were understated, but it became a glue that often held us together. She had been willing to step in and stay in a new culture, in a family's home far away from her own, and in difficult hospital settings. But now it was time for her to head home to Kenya.

The day after Senge left us, Geoffrey developed a fever. We cringed, knowing what it meant: We had to go to the ER, and Geoffrey would be admitted. We knew this because we had already lived it with Ryan. We didn't want to go back, but we had to. Mel drove Geoffrey and me to UCLA while Titus and Mama Micah stayed with the other three.

The next day, as Geoffrey played in his airplane bed, the culture reports came back. Geoffrey was growing salmonella—a common but dangerous organism for transplant patients—in his central line. A different round of IV antibiotics was started.

We weren't going home anytime soon.

On the same day, Mel received word his dad in Australia was dying, so he, Mary, and Micah flew to Australia that night. We all felt the shift of Senge's absence and the Herberts rightly needing to be on the other side of the world.

Mary called in the troops—as she would say—to walk alongside us, wherever possible.

I lived the next seven days with Geoffrey at UCLA while Titus worked to hold down the fort at the house with Sharon, Ella, and Ryan.

Geoffrey and I played with dinosaurs, read books, and tried to pass the time, the monotony of days and nights in the hospital once more. We were tired of the hospital, the stays that felt never-ending. I understood the fragility of Geoffrey's immune system and the complexity of his healing. There was need for caution.

More and more investigations were done, trying to put the puzzle pieces together of what was happening with Geoffrey. An

MRI came back showing osteomyelitis, infection in the bones of Geoffrey's lower legs.

Would the vicious cycle ever end?

One day, his IV pump was beeping after his antibiotic infusion was completed. I pushed the call light. "Mrs. Kiplagat, this is Mary. How may I help you?"

To most of our team, the different surnames didn't make sense. I just responded to whatever name was called out.

Never mind.

"Mary, it's raining here," I said.

"Excuse me, honey?"

Laughing at my tired shell-of-a-self, I clarified, "Mary, it's beeping in here."

"Alright, Mrs. Kiplagat, your nurse will be right in."

The months and months of beeping led me to ask myself many a time why the beeping occurs in the patient's room.

The purpose of every beeping was to notify or raise alarm to the nurse who was almost never in the room when the beeping took place. Why couldn't the beeping occur on a device the nurse held versus in the room where the patient and family weren't allowed to do anything about it?

And why in a wireless world did everything still require wires in the hospital?

This ongoing internal dialogue may have been part of the reason why it was "raining" in our room.

With Geoffrey, the nurses no longer called us mom and dad when they walked into the room. All the regulars on the floor felt like friends, and they called us by name. They knew we were worn, and their kindness with our tired selves helped us through each shift.

As Geoffrey watched shows on the iPad in his airplane bed, another dose of IV antibiotics was flowing through his veins. A news report popped up on my computer screen. A fire was growing in my hometown. My parents and sister's family still lived there.

A small fire, started by a spark from a trailer, was growing in size and intensity. It burned in the more rural lake area, but the smoke poured everywhere and seemed to be approaching town. The dry, hot valley of Redding created a perfect storm for the fire, making it nearly impossible for the firefighters to contain it.

* * *

Geoffrey was discharged on the day the Herberts returned from Australia. Meanwhile, the fire continued to grow in Redding. I was relieved to see Mel when he came to pick us up from UCLA, but his words were a painful reality, "I've been to Australia and back, and you're still in the same spot."

As I watched the news long into the night, it felt like our family—though many miles away from the fire—was unraveling. We were exhausted and spent.

Geoffrey didn't want to go to sleep, traumatized from hospital life. He wanted attention but also space, a tenuous balancing act.

Ella was melting in ways I'd never seen before. She has always had a big personality and a strong will, but this was different. She was regressing developmentally, wanting me to hold her like she was going to be nursed. She'd kick and scream uncontrollably, throwing herself onto the floor.

My closeness made her feel safe, but it took hours to quiet her troubled spirit. It was a form of grief that was guttural, and I felt it in every fiber of my heart.

"I don't want to do this anymore," she'd yell. "I want to go home to Kenya, and I can't even remember it anymore." Tears streamed down her face.

"Oh, Ella. I want to go home too, but we aren't ready yet," was all I could say.

Ella articulated what we all felt. It had become too much. But we weren't done.

Neither Titus nor I, though, wanted Ella to be broken in our fight for healing for the boys.

* * *

I lay in bed at 2 a.m., watching the news. The fires raged through Redding, and it felt like there were fires raging around us.

Ella was asleep, nestled in between Titus and me. She woke up earlier in the night screaming from a night terror. I took her outside under the night sky. Holding her tight, I assured her it would be okay.

I hoped it was true.

I was weary in a way that scared me. Like Ella, I didn't want to do it anymore. I wanted an easier way. I wanted her and all of us to feel safe again.

But what if this didn't get better? Would it always be like this?

There weren't landmarks to signal that we were on the right path. The distance, as far as I could see, was still dark.

As we tried to manage the exhaustion and grief from the toll of chronic disease, from the frequent hospitalizations, another firestorm came just days later.

There was confusion and sadness within our little ones as to why Mama and Geoffrey had to go back to the hospital... again.[27]

There were heartbreaking questions, "Do you have to stay? Again? Can I come too?"

There were tears that followed.

Healing was on its way, but it needed more time.

---

27 On several more occasions, Geoffrey was admitted to the hospital for grueling weeks at a time. Living through that reality was hard on all of us. It may be hard on you, too, so I'll spare you the details.

22

Sun-Friend

"Sun-friend is following me," Geoffrey said with delight during a moment of play sandwiched between rest and another scary dressing change.

Having been in and out of the hospital, we were finally home again. But there was a lot of "choking" these days. Like clockwork, Geoffrey would vomit in the morning. It was most likely related to the high-dose antibiotics he was on, but perhaps it was also a bit from GvHD.

At breakfast time, Geoffrey would need to throw up, and Mama Micah would move in quickly to take care of him and to "clean up on aisle five," as she often referred to it.

Healing takes time. It takes patience. A waxing and waning between health and wholeness and just not quite yet. A hope of freedom to play outside with siblings and the reality that Geoffrey's body temperature wouldn't autoregulate in the heat. A desire to swim with siblings or even take a bath and the reality of a central line that didn't allow for it.

But this little boy continued to imagine, drawing us further into his story.

He often talked of Stellaluna, the bat from one of his favorite books. He even attempted echolocation while in the ER. He wanted to talk to Ryan or Ella, so he yelled, "Echo, echolocation, Ella! Echo, echolocation, Ryan!"

Geoffrey referred to the sun and moon as his sun-friend and moon-friend. He loved to watch the sun set and the moon rise. And as the sun left us each day, he told us it was traveling back to Kenya and instructed it to greet his brothers and sisters.

"Say hi to Alice and Rose. Good-bye, sun-friend."

* * *

Back at home, I walked to the park with Geoffrey. As I pushed him in his stroller, we talked about the big trees. We pointed out the different shapes and sizes of the houses along the streets. "It's a beautiful neighborhood, isn't it?" I said.

Without missing a beat, this little boy who didn't speak English only a year ago said, "I know a song like that." And he began to sing the song he undoubtedly learned from Mama Micah, who basically is a female version of Mr. Rogers. She is thoughtful and kind, and she knows well how to do all things related to kids. I watched in awe as she'd navigate each day with our children.

"It's a beautiful day in this neighborhood, a beautiful day for a neighbor. Would you be mine? Could you be mine?" Geoffrey sang with a thoughtful smile. "Won't you be my neighbor?"

Tears filled my eyes. I heard the song anew; the questions were an invitation.

This little boy now had a hundred percent of his sister's DNA living and growing inside of him, in cells that had found their home within Geoffrey. And in doing so, sickle cell disease miraculously became part of his past, not present, medical history.

* * *

By nature, and by habit, I am a planner. I like to be organized, have things well thought through and coordinated. I pay attention to details. Most of the time, this is a strength, but this season did not leave room—physically or emotionally—to get too far ahead of the moment, hour, and day.

On many days, the unpredictability of the boys' health and treatment made tomorrow a distant future.

Since we were still in Los Angeles, finding a school for the girls was on Titus' and my list of things to figure out. We were trying to decide on a couple of nearby schools and walked into the office of one. We asked for an enrollment packet for kindergarten and one for fifth grade.

I wasn't sure how much more I needed to say—or not say—about our journey, as we didn't have all the supporting residency documents the school district required. We weren't homeowners, nor were we renters. We didn't have an electricity bill in our name.

Our story was that we moved in with friends for a year while our two boys from Kenya were getting bone marrow transplants at UCLA to cure them of sickle cell disease. Their twelve-year-old sister was their matched sibling donor. The kids' parents died two years ago, a few months apart. Their dad in a roadside accident. Their mom in childbirth. The baby miraculously survived. He was brought to the hospice—yes, we help to run a hospice in a rural village—when he was five days old. That was our introduction to the kids. Yes, we had traveled with these three children as well as our four-year-old biological daughter.

I did not say any of this, because I was standing in a school office finding it difficult to believe my own story. As I floundered a bit to try and find the right pieces of our journey to tell the secretary, the principal came out of her office and introduced herself.

Before I could say anything, with tears in her eyes, she said, "I know you. I know your story. I go to Christian Assembly."

In that moment, God's kindness was palpable. In a city of ten million people, I happened to walk into a school where a principal went to my home church. She knew who I was. She knew our story.

I was surprised to be known, to not need to explain, to not have to fight to get help or access for my kids. In my soul, I felt the beautiful words of Jesus reminding me anew, "If I take care of the birds, I will take care of you."

The girls didn't end up going to this school, but it was a moment where I felt seen. My planning, as necessary as it may be sometimes, didn't create this.

Even in my prayers, I had not known to ask for such a gift, but it was given anyway.

* * *

I rushed home from the hospital for back-to-school night for the girls. Geoffrey was in good hands with Mama Micah by his side, and Ryan stayed home playing with Baba Micah.

Titus, the girls, and I headed to a new school for a picnic and the chance to meet their teachers. They would begin school in a few days.

Before approaching Sharon's homeroom teacher, Ms. Miranda, I asked Sharon, "How do you want me to introduce you? Is it okay if I say that you're my daughter?"

"Yeah, it's okay."

We waited in line to say hello. Before I could begin, Sharon confidently said, "Hi, Ms. Miranda. My name is Sharon, and this is my mom."

Her words were generous. I smiled at Sharon, both proud and humbled.

* * *

On the first day of school, Sharon started middle school at a public charter school down the street. As we walked, she sang, "I just can't wait to go to school," to the tune of *The Lion King*. There was so much excitement and desire to learn within her. We prayed as we walked.

When we reached the gate of the school, I asked her if she wanted me to go in with her. She said no and gave me a big hug. I walked away.

I arrived back to get Ella ready to start kindergarten. It was a bit of a rough morning for her, and by the time I reached home she had decided to cancel kindergarten. Thankfully, she recovered fairly quickly and had a great first day of school.

Titus, Ryan, and I accompanied her to her kindergarten breakfast.

The nervous energy from all the little ones and the emotion from the parents felt tangible. School offered a new and wonderful adventure, and I was so excited for all that Ella was going to learn.

When asked by her teacher what my expectations were for Ella this year, I replied, "I want her to grow in kindness and respect. I want her to do her best."

A big highlight of the morning was how much Ryan loved being at school with us. He so rarely got to leave the house except to go to the hospital, but on this Monday, I carried him on my back to take his sister to school.

On this same Monday morning, I traveled back down to UCLA to be with Geoffrey. Mama Micah had taken the night shift, allowing us to accompany the girls to school.

Geoffrey was scheduled to go in for another MRI with sedation later in the day. The team wanted to see if there might be an infection in his arm bones too. New spots had shown up within the bones of his legs, complicating his treatment.

Geoffrey was tired. We were tired. And there were important investigations still to be done and decisions to be made. Steps that felt tenuous. Answers that couldn't come easily. While I didn't know what was ahead, I chose to believe that God held this little boy in his hands.

* * *

September rolled around, marking an entire year of the Kenyans—the way Mel referred to us—living at the Herbert home.

We began to look at the days by where we were a year ago. Arriving in Los Angeles with the notion we would only be staying in the yellow house for a couple of weeks. As we remembered, we began to laugh about some aspects of the journey. We were no longer in the waiting-for-transplants-to-come period.

We joked about writing two parallel books. Ours would be *The Year We Moved In*. Theirs, *The Year They Moved In*.

A new season was upon us. Micah and our high schoolers left for college. One by one, they came to say good-bye. We were all marked by the friendship, the sense of family created by the most surprising little community that helped to carry us many a mile.

The girls were thriving in school. Sharon's teacher chose her to receive the Shining Star Award, commenting that she wished every student could have even a little bit of Sharon's hunger to learn.

And our Ella was given the Cooperation Award, which might be one of my proudest moments in life thus far. Cooperation would not be the first word I would use to describe Ella, but thankfully she was finding her way in school, loving routine, her teacher, and new friends.

Even if only for a few months, I was grateful they were given the opportunity to engage and learn, to shine and cooperate.

* * *

Light was coming back into Ryan's eyes as he was weaned off all his medicines and the port was removed from his chest. He wasn't talking yet, but he was very much alive.

Geoffrey finally got through the infections and was also able to stop medications, one by one, until he wasn't on any. His lines were removed, and he celebrated by swimming and taking numerous baths.

There wasn't one single moment when I realized we were out of the dark. It was more of a steady trudge that many a day felt as if it would never end. One foot in front of the other, over and over again. Through the muck and mire. Through valleys that were as dark as death. Through mountains treacherous and nearly insurmountable.

And then suddenly, we were in a new place, looking back at where we had come from. Recalling the details, the traumas. Pondering how it happened at all.

The follow-up doctor visits at UCLA were getting spaced out further and soon enough, there was talk of going home. A date selected, plane tickets were bought.

23

Home

Piles of children's clothes and toys lay scattered throughout the Herberts' house. Some were waiting to be packed in a suitcase to accompany us home. Others would find another child to warm or befriend.

While I am not usually sentimental about belongings, these items journeyed with us through some tough and wonderful days. Toys gave our children the opportunity to heal as they played.

Hopper—Geoffrey's stuffed animal with a line coming from its chest—was both a toy and a tool we used to teach our kids about their central lines. It helped them be less afraid, to normalize what felt so often anything but normal.

I placed the little gray moccasins that held Ryan's feet as he learned to walk again into the duffle bag. Beside them was his navy-blue beanie that had covered his bald head all those days in the PICU.

The soft hospital blankets and heart banner would all make their way back to Kenya, reminders of moments both hard and wonderful.

Twelve teddy bears wearing pink and blue scrubs were evidence of when one of our boys and Sharon had made trips to the OR. Each represented a time I let go of Ryan, Geoffrey, or Sharon and trusted that it was for the best, always in the hope it was leading toward life. They represented the relief I felt when another bear was found accompanying one of my kids on their hospital beds after surgery, that we had survived another step in a series of many.

We didn't know there would be *that* many steps, that it would take *this* long, that we would need all the love we received to carry us day and night.

There were mounds of children's books read over and again while one or more of our children filled someone's lap.

Micah, Alexa, Hayden, and Harrison were just a few of the high schoolers who took the time to read *Go Dog. Go!* or *Little Blue Truck* to Geoffrey or Ella, and *In My New Yellow Shirt* to Ryan. There was *Snuggle Puppy of Mine*, a story for which we made a song up and sang on repeat until it felt like everyone else should know the song too.

Sharon's artwork, representing hours upon hours of labor and delight, growth and development, filled a hard-sided suitcase. Deep and loving friendships had been formed around the wonder of creating—something that had not been a part of Sharon's world before.

People like Ms. Jaye and her team at the art studio held Sharon's story, loving her and knowing details about a young girl from the other side of the planet. Sharon tasted the joy, processed grief of loss, and the longing for home within her work.

How do you pack all of that away, holding the marvel of it? They cried with her, laughed together, dreamed of what it might look like to go home. And these beautiful expressions captured it, one paintbrush stroke at a time.

Just when I thought I was almost done with the sorting and packing, I'd find more toys tucked in here or there. Some were broken. This journey had been messy. Not everything had a proper place to land. Not all endured the turbulence of months of unpredictability where we simply were trying to survive. Evidence of a story that wasn't all pretty and put together.

So much was outside of our control, but a thread held it together—the generosity from hundreds of different hands that stopped by to bring a book, a puzzle, a stuffed animal. Everyone yearned for life and healing for our boys, and also wanted us to know we were cared for along the way.

*　*　*

"When are we going to do Alice's treatment?" Sharon asked with a look of understanding in her eyes. It wasn't an easy question. She already knew there was not an answer, but she asked anyway.

"Sharon, we don't have a match for Alice," I told her again.

"Can we do the test again?" she asked. "I want to give her my bone marrow." It wasn't that she had an urge to save Alice herself. She simply wanted Alice to be saved. We sat together with the hard unknowns and wondered if God would do for Alice what he did for Geoffrey and Ryan.

Now, we felt more and more what I could not fully hold on the day I received the report, the day we learned that Alice lacked a match.

We had walked the hard miles that led to our little boys' freedom from this disease. And we will still walk, whatever it may look like for Alice to suffer with it.

Even from the other side of the world, we knew there were days when Alice curled up in a ball and cried. "*Mgongo*," she would whisper, my back. "*Mkono*," my hand. It started with a whimper and would grow louder as the intensity in pain that my body cannot understand, increased.

One day, Alice will sit beside the two little boys who no longer hurt. Like a mother who forgets the pain of labor, they cannot remember, thankfully, what the hurt was like.

Her suffering is her own, yes. But it is also shared by us. We hold it and ache.

When we left for Los Angeles with the boys, I didn't have space to wrestle with the why. I did not ask the questions that don't have answers.

Why them and not her?

I did not know how to hold all of this in my heart. Honestly, I thought little about it. It wasn't that I didn't know or care. I did. But my limited mind space was consumed and maxed out with what we had—an opportunity to save two brothers. My mind could not make room, then, for what we did not have.

Love was there, yes, but would it be enough to carry us through so many unknowns? Through heartache and disappointment?

And then months into the journey, I lay beside Geoffrey in his hospital airplane bed while he received chemotherapy; and seemingly out of the blue, he prayed one night, "God, heal Alice." And then night after night, he remembered her in his prayers.

There was space but not answers—at least that we knew of—for Alice. Geoffrey's prayers were a simple ongoing plea from a little boy enduring his own struggle to live. I laid beside him and allowed my heart to enlarge to make more room for her.

* * *

As time went by, Geoffrey forgot much of Kenya, and it was hard to witness. Ella had words for this loss. "Mama, I miss our home in Kenya. I miss my friends. There's so much I can't even remember anymore." The loss troubled her. But Geoffrey couldn't remember the details of his prior home or why he lived with us instead of his mom and dad.

"Geoffrey, I don't know if you remember, but when you were little, you had a different mama," I explained as he played in the bathtub, "and she died. That is how you came to live with us." (I tell you, those types of conversations seriously need to come with an instruction manual. How do you explain something like this to a little boy?)

"Oh," brief pause, "I don't remember that." He continued to play with his dinosaur, Chomp.

As months passed, Geoffrey's memories were less and less overt and more hidden in concepts, many of which I did not have context for. What became utterly clear was that Alice represented *home* for him.

When Geoffrey dreamed of Kenya, he thought of her.

As Christmas approached and we asked Geoffrey what he wanted as a gift, his list contained stuffed animal flamingos. One for him, and one for Alice.

* * *

In the same way Geoffrey didn't remember that his mom had died, Ella didn't remember either. As we prepared to return to Kenya, she talked about how Geoffrey and Sharon would come for sleepovers but go back to living with their mom.

I tried to gently correct her for a season, telling her, "No, they're going to still live with us." But her little mind couldn't grab ahold of it all.

Titus and I sat with Ella one evening and explained, "Ella, I don't think you remember, but Geoffrey and Sharon's mama died. They're going to still live with us when we get home to Kenya." (She wasn't yet willing to accept that Ryan didn't come from my belly. And so, we left that conversation for another day.)

Her eyes grew wide and filled with tears, "Oh, no," she said.

We sat together quietly as her mind and heart began to shift from her expectations to our new reality.

* * *

As we were preparing to leave, Mama Micah gifted us with a book she had painted and beautifully written. She entitled it *Love's Journey* and inscribed these words, "To my dear Kenyans, may this book help you remember our amazing journey together. I love you all so very much, Mama Micah."

I didn't know, on the first day we met how long the journey would feel as you left your village to travel down a bumpy road through red-earthed hills, as sun-friend followed you, lighting the way through the airport and beyond...

I didn't know how we would find each other, separated by language and tradition, speaking only LOVE as we navigated our days.

With moon-friend sent to us from afar, to delight our nights.

I didn't know where you would sleep, or how long you would stay with us, under one roof, eating and singing and breathing together as sun-friend rose over us day after day.

I didn't know how hard it would be to sit with the pain and suffering that comes from bodies not fully perfect and in need of help.

I knew only that you were sent to us by love, and that anywhere you would be, we would be there together. And as sun-friend rose and moon-friend shone from Kenya and back each day, we would be carried by love, in prayers and deeds until it was time for a journey to end. And you would travel back over the sea and down the bumpy road to your village in the green hills. And you would send back to me sun-friend at the end of each day. And I would send you moon-friend. And love will circle the whole world until we are close together again!

* * *

Ella and Geoffrey sang as we finished packing the last of the suitcases, "What are you thankful for?" It was a random children's song they had heard on some YouTube channel with nursery rhymes. Ella, not surprisingly, sang with the same vigor and volume with which she lives her life.

"What are you thankful for?" she shouted. The answer was undoubtedly *so very much*. As the suitcases were weighed and filled the van, "What are you thankful for?" was heard being sung in the background.

* * *

Mel and Titus rode together in one car while Mama Micah drove the kids and me in another. A nervous energy filled the air, along with a mix of emotions.

We felt excitement as we were finally returning to our village in the green hills in Kenya, and also overwhelming sadness as this chapter that had brought us all together was coming to an end—at least in the way we had been living it for so many months.

None of us could have imagined 477 days earlier all that would fill the days and nights of this journey. The weeks and months that blurred together were made up of sacrifice and love. So many early mornings and late nights we met up in the kitchen, reflecting on the day or the season, trying to make sense of it all.

I would sometimes say to Mel and Mary, "Thank you for choosing to do this with us, for saying yes to all of this."

Mel would smirk, "We didn't know what we were signing up for," which was altogether true. And yet, they stayed in the mire, in the mess, every step of the way.

We were all marked invariably by the suffering required for healing to come. By the darkness that swallowed us up, but as we stayed there—in the scariest of places—new life was born. In the marrow of two little boys. In the hearts of all of us who dared to believe they were worth whatever the journey might cost.

* * *

The 405 freeway was congested as we drove it one final time. We passed by the exit to UCLA on our way to the airport. We had driven this same way over and over again in the past fifteen months. It felt surreal. *Did all of this really happen?* At times, we lived a horrific nightmare. On this side of it, a dream come true. An answer to prayer upon prayer.

A convoy of vehicles accompanied us to the airport. One final demonstration of how the Herberts and their friends always show up, capturing the magic of what it looks like when a community of strangers, for the sake of love, become family.

We stood as a group in front of the elevator doors where the six of us would go ahead, returning to a land we knew as home, though our little ones could barely remember it. What they knew now is a yellow home in Woodland Hills that welcomed us as if we belonged there.

Mama and Baba Micah, who walked every single step alongside us for 477 days, would stay behind. Their love carried us, and now we were giving final hugs. Ella's brown eyes looked at Mama Micah's tear-stained face, and she became still for a moment, unsure of what to say.

"Don't cry, Mama Micah," Geoffrey said as he held on tightly for as long as possible to the mama who had welcomed him into her world. And by doing so, she discovered the wonder of his. Sharon leaned into Mama H. as the sadness of saying good-bye gripped her soul. It was time to go home, but she also understood she was returning changed by the journey.

We paused for one last moment, drinking it all in. In a season where so often I felt at a loss for words, I whispered, "This is what love looks like."

When the glass elevator doors closed behind us, we were still waving and blowing kisses, brushing away tears on both sides of the door.

We worked our way through TSA with wiggly little ones. Laptops and liquids, our jackets, and shoes were placed on the trays. One by one, we walked through the X-ray machine and made our way to the gate where a plane headed to Paris already awaited us.

Are we really going home? All six of us?

The answer still brings tears to my eyes and a smile to my face. Those months ago, while we sat in the PICU and waited, my chest tight with grief and fear, a different kind of tears had flowed. Oh,

I hoped new life would come. But it felt as if death would take away our boy, stealing this dream and any future we might have with him. I recalled the many nights Geoffrey called out from his airplane bed, "I am not going to get better."

We arrived at this moment through the shadows of death and despair. We planted ourselves, and stayed there, for as long as it took. Without a promise or certitudes of the path that would lead us home.

Ryan's diseased bone marrow had died, as had Geoffrey's. Death was their path to new life. As life formed anew and as signs appeared, we held onto those gently. Not smashing or squelching them as they needed time to germinate and take root. They needed nourishing, day by day and hour by hour.

I still don't believe the purpose of my children's suffering was to teach me compassion, but compassion certainly has been a side effect. Alongside a beautiful community, I labored for my children with all the love and courage I possessed. Imperfectly but wholeheartedly.

* * *

Nelson Mandela once wrote, "There is no easy walk to freedom anywhere, and many of us will have to pass through the valley of the shadow of death again and again before we reach the mountaintop of our desires."[28] This was certainly true for us.

In seat 18C en route to Paris, I was surrounded by our little family. Ryan sat on Titus' lap, squirming, restless from the long flight. I picked him up and placed him into the same purple Ergo baby carrier that held him on so many occasions before.

---

28   Nelson Mandela, *No Easy Walk to Freedom* (London: Penguin Books, 2003).

I looked around the plane and smiled as if I carried a secret. Those around us did not know the wonder that filled me because of this fussy toddler I tried to calm.

I stood in the galley and swayed back and forth, stroking Ryan's face and hair. His skin was now smooth, hiding how hard the fight truly had been. His beautiful eyelashes were filling in, along with his freshly cut black hair. No visible traces of the battle. I rocked side to side until his eyelids grew heavy, and he drifted off to sleep.

I walked back up the narrow aisle to row 18 where Geoffrey and Ella were sound asleep in their seats. I handed our sleeping little boy back to Titus, and with a catch in my throat, I leaned over to him. "It is everything we hoped for."

All six of us getting to go home.

What are you thankful for? The answer was *so very much.*

* * *

We landed in Nairobi on an early morning flight, before the sun would paint the night sky in hues of orange.

Titus' countenance shifted visibly—the months of longing for home were over. He could finally take a deep breath in and exhale, relaxing in a way I had not seen while away. We slowly made our way through the warm, balmy terminal to the immigration line.

It was my turn to be the non-citizen. My turn to be the one questioned for my coming, for the intention of travel. And in true Kenyan hospitality, the immigration agent stamped our passports, adding, "*Karibuni nyumbani.*" Welcome home.

* * *

After a local flight and two hours of driving, we took the familiar tarmac road from Eldoret to the red dirt road that would lead us to our home.

How could we even begin to appreciate all the miles covered in the last fifteen months? We had left this place with a hope and a dream for the boys to have a chance to live free from the disease that had threatened them daily.

We returned holding the miracle of their healing. There hadn't been a magic button to take the pain away. Rather, it was a slow and deliberate path that led from death to new life.

The road twisted and turned through the green hills. I knew each of them by heart, and now my feet would touch the ground once more. As we approached our little orange home, the African sun was setting. "Say hi to Mama Micah," Geoffrey said, sending sun-friend back to America, to a land and people who had loved us so well.

I heard the sound of singing long before I saw the sea of faces—hundreds of our neighbors gathered to line the dirt road leading to our home. The sounds of their celebration and rejoicing surrounded us from all sides, carrying us across the threshold. One lady sang out a verse in acapella, and the crowd followed in a call and response style, accompanied by dancing and ululation.

Tears of joy flooded our faces. A myriad of memories led us to this moment. They flashed through my head as I scanned the crowd to see the individual faces of all ages and sizes.

Mama Chumba, the aunt to our children, with tears streaming down her face, scooped up Geoffrey. Their embrace was tender and sweet. When Ella saw Mama Jesang, a lady who has helped to care for her since she was a tiny baby, she dropped from my arms to jump into hers. Deep love passed between them.

Titus carried Ryan tightly to his chest, our son, the little king who first came to us in his pink blanket. As he sang and danced, Ryan remained in his safe place, the strong arms of his baba.

Sharon stood close by my side—eyes wide open, singing along. She gave so much of herself, making new life a possibility, and now a reality.

We were paraded toward the gate, hugging each person along the way. In a wonderful role reversal, Kibet had walked from his home to ours to receive us. He looked me in the eyes and held my hand, "*Karibu*, Mama Ella."

Years earlier, I had committed to walk alongside him as he fought to survive. Now, he was doing the same for me and my family, celebrating victory with us.

When we reached our gate, Alice stood in the middle of the crowd waiting to welcome us. We were divided by a ceremonial blue and pink ribbon strung across the gateway. Once we cut the ribbon, we would officially be home.

Geoffrey did not wait for the ribbon to be cut. He crawled under the moment he spotted Alice.

Night after night, Geoffrey had sent sun-friend to greet Alice. For him, Kenya was never referenced without including her. And now, they were back together. She was his home, and they hugged one another with a love deeper and wider than oceans. All was not perfect nor was it complete. But they were together, and for now, that was enough.

We cut the ribbon and danced and sang among a crowd of witnesses. The extravagant welcome was a gift to our weary bodies and souls. Another moment where time could have stood still to tell us once more: *This is what love looks like.* A message of "well done" being poured out like salve upon our healing wounds.

Now. Here. This.

Four hundred and eighty days earlier, we drove away with a dream of freedom from sickle cell for our boys. In some ways, it seemed to be an invitation that was as hard as it was sacred.

Thankfully, we only knew in part then what we now know more fully.

There was a question that guided us. It sat on the shelf in Mama Micah's house, painted on a wooden sign. It simply read: What if?

What if the God who is able to do the impossible chose to do it once more?

What if brave love was the requirement and also the reward?

And what happens when the guiding question begins to shift from *what if* to *why not?*

It is here our frailties and limitations are exposed and also set free to love.

For four hundred and eighty days, our hearts longed for home, while also finding a place more loving and kinder than we dared to imagine possible.

With the joyful sound of singing all around, I could finally see the path our dreaming made. And from beyond the skies, it led us safely home.

UPDATE

Daily, I watch Ryan, and in my mind's eye, I see through the lens of *this is what I would have missed.*

From up-close and far-away distances, I revel at the miracle of his life. All the mud pies. The early mornings he awakes to announce, "It's morning time!" The hugs where he tucks his arms inside rather than around so he can snuggle in tightly. The magical sound of his giggling that echoes throughout our home. The way he adores his brothers and sisters, through and through. "Me help you," he offers a few hundred times a day.

Ryan found his voice a few months after his third birthday, and his words and make-believe stories enchant me. All of this and so much more is what I was afraid to lose on those dark days in the hospital when healing felt another world away.

Celeste Ng captures with words what I hold within my soul: "To a parent, your child wasn't just a person: your child was a place, a kind of Narnia, a vast eternal place where the present you were living and the past you remembered and the future you longed for all at the same time."[29]

---

29 Celeste Ng, *Little Fires Everywhere* (New York: Penguin Random House, 2017).

I can see it—the past, present, and future—whenever I look at Ryan. I sometimes wonder if I saw it all on that first day we met at the hospice when my eyes beheld a little king swaddled in pink.

I see each of my children this way, through a filter of what was and is, of what I hope is still to come. For the boys, their wounds have turned into scars. Visible reminders on their skin, within their blood, written all over our hearts.

They used to have sickle cell disease.

Alice now lives with our family; she's one of us too. When I look at her, I see a past and a present filled with moments of normalcy intermixed with loss and untold pain.

Most days, I don't yet know how to see the future for her. But like Geoffrey, I find myself reaching for the courage to ask for Alice to have a gift of healing too.

Our family recently hiked up a mountain near our home. The path was steep and challenging, and I had low expectations that the seven of us would make it to the top.

I was worried Alice would develop a pain crisis with the change in altitude. I was concerned with how each step left her breathless. But she was not going to give up, even if she had to be carried up the mountain.

I also doubted Geoffrey would be able to climb with his spastic foot, and I kept asking over and over how he was doing, telling him, "Geoffrey, if you're tired, we can carry you."

He looked at me with a big smile. "It's not too easy, Mama," he said, "but we can do hard things."

Within weeks of us moving back to Kenya, Living Room opened a new forty-nine-bed hospital where we have a wing dedicated for children and their parents to come and receive cancer care and hospice services.

Each time I walk into the space where colorful quilts are spread across hospital beds and toys sit on a brightly painted shelf, I understand intimately that "we are bound by a common anguish," as Harper Lee described.[30]

I now see the pain and hope with well-acquainted eyes.

It isn't difficult for me to sit beside a mother anticipating the death of her child and to wonder how much it hurts. I remember sitting there too. I have also experienced in the dark the untellable love that carried our family through.

I want it for others in their suffering too.

After all, only love matters. And the invitation from beyond the skies is not yet over—it is always ready to stretch our hearts further still. Ready to put hands and feet to our love.

---

30   Casey Cep, "Why Harper Lee Struggled to Write a Book After *To Kill a Mockingbird*," Time, May 7, 2019. time.com/5584939/harper-lee-after-to-kill-a-mockingbird/.

YOU ARE INVITED

ong before my family's transplant journey, I helped to create
Living Room, a hospice in Kenya where men, women and
children come either to heal or to be loved until they die.

As a mother who has walked the long and scary road of suffering
with my own children, I understand even more intimately the
importance of Living Room's work.

With Chumba, one of our guests at Kimbilio Hospice

At Living Room, we walk alongside patients and families going through medical crisis and provide quality physical, emotional, and spiritual care every single day. To learn more about Living Room's loving work and ways you can get involved, please visit **LivingRoomInternational.org**.

I'd love to hear from my readers. You can reach me via email, Twitter, or Instagram at:

juli@frombeyondtheskies.com

@julimcgowanboit

@LivingRoomInternational

ACKNOWLEDGMENTS

Thank you doesn't begin to describe all I feel for the community of family and friends who have accompanied us on this journey. My hope is that the words of this book have given you a glimpse into how much your love mattered and helped to carry us. Honestly, I could fill an entire book simply by listing the names of everyone who has loved us along the way.

Thank you to Karen Anderson and the wonderful team at Morgan James for believing in me and choosing to publish this book. To Adele and Staci, thank you for gifting this story with your remarkable editorial talents. And to a group of trusted friends, thank you for graciously sifting through early pages and providing invaluable feedback.

Thank you to Mary, Mel, and Micah for making room in your home and hearts for us to "just come" and stay for 477 days. We will forever be grateful. Also, thank you for allowing your beautiful community to become ours. The names are many, but I want to mention a few: Mama and Baba H; our beloved high schoolers—Alexa, Hayden, Harrison, Henry, Matia, Christine, Max, Natalie, Scott, Robert, Bianca, Christian, Tyler, Zane, 2 Eddies, Carolina, Bella, and Cody; Cindy P.; Ms. Lundy; Ms. Jaye, Ms. Heidi, and Ms. Michelle; Ceci; Ray; the Masinis; Koko Debbie; and the EM:RAP team.

To Senge, we love you and will always be grateful for the ways you tenderly cared for our children. Mama Kathy, Sarah D., Sarah O., and Uncle Mosh—thank you for waiting through Advent with us. Travis and Kimberly, you have always been a safe place for us to tell our story. To Mark, Tom, and our entire Christian Assembly family, we are blessed beyond words to be followers of Jesus with you.

A special thanks to our Living Room leaders and staff who daily live out love in such bold and beautiful ways. It is my greatest privilege to serve alongside of you. Thank you to David and Allison Tarus, Peter and Janet Boit, Brian and Kristin Albright, and all of our neighbors who made it possible for Titus and me to step away. To all of Living Room's partners from around the globe, thank you for all of the ways you stand with us.

To the doctors and nurses in Kenya, Indiana, and Los Angeles who cared for our children, *thank you*. Our gratitude doesn't feel like it's enough, but it is what we have to give.

To our families, the Boits and McGowans, thank you for the lifetime of love and support you have lavished on us.

And finally, to my husband and children, thank you for allowing me to try and find words to tell our story. I love you more than you will ever know.

ABOUT THE AUTHOR

Titus and Juli with their "many" children

Juli Boit is the Founder and International Director of Living Room International, a non-profit providing hospice and palliative care services to adults and children in Kenya. She is a nurse practitioner who is challenged daily to learn more, listen better and love deeper. Juli lives in Kenya with her husband, Titus, and their children: Sharon, Alice, Ella, Geoffrey, and Ryan.

Learn more at **LivingRoomInternational.org**.

FROM

BEYOND

THE SKIES

———

THE REMARKABLE STORY OF LOVE, LOSS AND NEW LIFE FOUND IN THE DARK

For more photos and videos of the people and story of From Beyond the Skies please visit:

FROMBEYONDTHESKIES.COM

Enter the code:

INVITED

CONTINUE THE STORY— PASS IT ON!

Sign your name to this 'library card' and pass it on to a friend or loved one. Scan the QR code to add your name to the journey. Our goal is for this book to travel 9,490 miles (Eldoret, Kenya →LA). Let's spread this message of hope and healing beyond the skies.

FROM THE LIBRARY OF:

NAME
_ _

LOCATION
_ _

FROM THE HEART OF KENYA

DATE	BORROWER / LOCATION

FROMBEYONDTHESKIES.COM/SHARE